Cloud Serv
in a Month

Build a Successful Cloud Service Offering
for Small Business in 30 Days

Karl W. Palachuk

Great Little Book Publishing Co., Inc.
Sacramento, CA

www.greatlittlebook.com

Great Little Book Publishing Co., Inc.
Sacramento, CA

Cloud Services in a Month – Build a Successful Cloud Service Offering for Small Business in 30 Days
by Karl W. Palachuk

www.greatlittlebook.com

978-1-942115-54-0 (Paperback)

978-1-942115-55-7 (ebook)

Cloud Services in a Month

Build a Successful Cloud Service Offering for Small Business in 30 Days

Karl W. Palachuk

Table of Contents

Your Downloadable Content

This book includes additional downloads that you will find very helpful. These include Word and Excel files, and a few other goodies.

If you purchased this book from SMB Books or Great Little Book, you should have received a download link when your purchase was completed.

If you lost that or purchased from Amazon or another reseller, you can register at **www.SMBBooks.com**.

Please have your purchase receipt ready to register. You'll need the Order ID. If you purchased somewhere else, you'll need to forward proof of purchase to us.

Your feedback is always welcome.

Author's Preface

In some sense, this book was started in 2008 when I gathered my employees around the big table in front of the even bigger white board and said, "Let's create a cloud strategy."

Our goal was to design an offering we could sell to every client as the "core technology" that every business needs. We were in the fifth year of amazing success with Small Business Server 2003. The 2008 edition was about to be released. But I just didn't believe the product would last long after that.

The amazing success of SBS 2003 boils down to a very simple formula: We essentially sold the exact same project over and over and over again. Some clients had more CALs (client access licenses) and some had fewer CALs. Some had a larger server and some had a smaller one. But the core project was nearly identical.

Setting up small businesses on SBS was very much like operating a production line. Ka-chunk. Ka-chunk. Ka-chunk.

I had read Nicholas Carr's book *The Big Switch*, and I was convinced that "The Cloud" was our inevitable future. The only question was, how soon would it be ready for us?

At some level, we didn't know any more than anyone else about what the cloud was in 2007-2008. But we signed up for Zenith Infotech's cloud offering and went to their training. And we had had great success hosting web sites and email in hosted ("cloud") platforms.

So I was determined to simply plough ahead and make corrections as we went along. We had to define the cloud to our clients, and we had to execute well in order to make sure that those who adopted a cloud solution were not disappointed.

And we pulled it off! We converted our smallest fifteen clients in one month. Note, please, that we had a ten seat minimum before this move, so our smallest client was moving one server and ten seats to cloud alternatives.

Ironically, 2008 was the year I published the first edition of *Managed Services in a Month*. So, while my company was moving full force into cloud services, I released what would become the most popular book ever on managed services.

That fall, the U.S. housing market collapsed and the U.S. stock market imploded. SBS 2008 was release in the worst recession of our lifetime. It was a truly great product that never sold as well as it should have, simply because no one was buying much of anything.

And as the economy improved, SBS 2011 was released. But by 2011 we had found other alternatives for most of the functions of SBS. Most of our clients were now 100% in the cloud. So we ended up only selling SBS 2011 to the few clients who absolutely had to have something on site.

Best of all, for us, is that we built managed services into our cloud bundle from day one. It was never an add-on or after thought. When I read blogs or newsletters that said managed services was dead, I laughed out loud. All I could think of was that these authors didn't understand managed services or cloud services in any meaningful way.

SMB Pre-Day Events

In 2010, my SMB Nation Pre-Day seminar was about how to move to cloud services.

And 2011.

And 2012, 2013, 2014, and 2015. In 2016 I did the Fall Pre-Day in association with SMB TechFest – on cloud services. There are many members of our community that have seen me present this business model FIVE or more times.

The sad truth is that I was presenting to people whose net operating profit was between five and fifteen per cent while ours was consistently around 60-75%. I got deeper and deeper into my model, but people still didn't convert. I honestly never understood why.

Finally, in 2017 I put on a world-wide roadshow with six hours of material that literally gave click-by-click instructions on how to design, bundle, implement, and manage the Cloud Five-Pack™ formula we had been using for years. I presented this material in twenty-five cities in the U.S., England, Ireland, Scotland, and Australia.

And that brings us to this book.

This book is intended to give you the latest version of the Cloud Five-Pack™, including massive supplemental materials (checklists, forms, client memos, etc.).

And like its big brother *Managed Services in a Month* (MSIAM), this book is designed to help you get off your butt and actually, create, implement, and sign your first cloud service bundle.

As always, I don't make any attempt to cover every single alternative out there. I can't, because I don't know all those things. I only cover what I know and what I believe. I use brand names as I see fit. On some other front (speaking, advertising, etc.) I have done business with one or more brands mentioned. But I haven't received a penny from anyone to be mentioned in this book or receive favorable treatment.

Cloud Services in a Month is intended to help everyone who wants to be a cloud service provider (CSP). If you've been doing Break/Fix or managed services, it will probably be easier to make the shift. Well, to be honest, it will be hard to change your mindset but easier to make the actual transition.

For those who are totally new to I.T. consulting, the mindset piece should be easy. But starting with no clients always makes it more difficult to adopt a program and make it successful right away. But you CAN do it! In fact, to be honest, you don't really have any choice.

I believe the basic model described here is your business model for at least the next five years, or more.

In the third edition of MSIAM (2018), I gave a quick overview of the Cloud Five-Pack™ bundle and how you can build a cloud offering. This book goes into all the details.

Choose Your Path

Although this remains a small-ish book, it will attempt to help three different groups of people, all on different paths. First, this book will help people who are just getting started in "computer consulting" and the technology business. Second, it will help established business owners move to a cloud services/managed services model.

Third, this book will help anyone – new or established – develop a cloud service offering specifically focused on the small business market. I'm not going to try to address every cloud offering out there or help you build a data center. But I will cover the design and delivery of basic cloud services.

Since 2008, we have sold a package of cloud services called the "Cloud Five-Pack™." I'll walk you through what that is, how you can design your own, and why you *should* be selling something like this going forward.

People always ask me if they can just buy Cloud Five-Pack™ services from me to sell to their customers. No. I don't have a way to do that, and you'll see why: It's too easy. If you stick me in the middle, you'll make less money and make it more complicated.

Just go make a bunch of money and leave me out of it!

A Note About KPEnterprises and Small Biz Thoughts

For sixteen years I owned and operated KPEnterprises Business Consulting, which has been the model for my experiences and writing over the last decade. But people and businesses evolve.

In 2011, my service manager bought out KPEnterprises and the KPEnterprises brand is now simply a brand name underneath Great Little Book Publishing Co., Inc. I am spending most of my time writing, consulting, and training technology consultants.

The consulting business became America's Tech Support (ATS), and I worked there for a few years. I worked as the Senior Systems Engineer for ATS. I was responsible for strategic planning, some sales, some project management, and some network migrations.

Then, in 2014 I started consulting on my own again under the Small Biz Thoughts brand. At the end of 2016 that business had grown and was taking too much time. So I sold it as well. I am now a coach and do backup tech support for the new owner.

And, as you'll see in this book, I have residual income from managing cloud services for many former clients. This mix works great for me. I get to play with new technology. I get to interact with clients. I get to keep my fingers in the support side of the business.

So . . . when I refer to KPEnterprises or Small Biz Thoughts in this book, I am either referring to the company I owned for sixteen years, ATS, SBT, or my current arrangement. All of these operated on the principles and guidelines discussed in this book.

I hope you find this little book useful. I welcome your feedback. Send me an email at **karlp@smallbizthoughts.com**. Let me know how you're doing.

Please also take a minute to connect with me on Twitter, Facebook, and LinkedIn. Just search for "KarlPalachuk" or Karl Palachuk on any of those services.

Also look for my SOP (standard operating procedure) videos on YouTube. I have well over 500 videos at www.youtube.com/smallbizthoughts.

Note:

_____

_____

_____

_____

_____

_____

_____

_____

I. Everyone's a Cloud Service Provider

1. Tiptoe into the Clouds?

When I train IT consultants (or write books), my "big theme" is always very practical: How can I help you *make* more money and *keep* more money? When I attend conferences, I'm often frustrated by vendors who only want to talk about "feature, feature, feature." I want to hear how I make money selling their product.

I'm honestly not trying to sell you anything in this book, but I want to show you how we make money and how I have sold millions of dollars' worth of cloud services over the course of the last 11 years. So, we're going to start talking about the cloud in general and then some of the specific ways that it fits into the SMB (small and medium business) space. After that, we'll cover the specific cloud offering that we put together and how it's evolved over the years. Finally, we'll talk more generally about the kinds of things you can be doing in the cloud.

Along the way, we'll have lots of specifics and "click-by-click" integration information. Be sure to download the supplemental materials! There are some checklists that get into quite a bit of detail about getting clients on board and so forth.

Zero-Based Thinking

I would encourage you to have what I call a zero-based view of this. Way back in the 1980s, they had something called *zero-based budgeting*. The idea was to take a fresh look at budgets. Instead of making incremental improvements based on where we are today, the theory went, let's assume we start at zero: Would we create this program? And if so, at what level would we fund it?

That's what I would like you to think about in terms of technology. If you were young, just graduated from high school, and you're trying to figure out what to do, would you create the business you have today? And what would you sell? How would you bundle it? How would you price it? And who would you sell it to?

There's a great product called ClickFunnels, developed by a guy named Russell Brunson. ClickFunnels is a marketing product, and he explains how it works in a book called *DotCom Secrets*.

Brunson says that, when you go out to market something, you should do a couple of things. One of them is you should be *an attractive character* or have an attractive character as your symbol.

Think about a company that has Ronald McDonald or Jack Box (the big ping pong ball head) for Jack in the Box. You should have an attractive character that you can put your marketing around and you should also have an *ideal client*.

Before you spend a nickel on trying to sell anything, it's very important that you know who your client is, because if you sell to the wrong clients you won't sell very much and it'll just frustrate you.

What does that mean for cloud services? Simple: When we talk about what we're going to do going forward, you may be looking at different clients as well as different products. That's an important thing to keep in mind. You may be rebuilding your business from the ground up.

Zero-based thinking . . . Look at everything with fresh eyes!

Handout: Change Plan

At the end of this book, I've left a few lined pages in case you need them. In the download materials that accompany this book you'll find a Change Plan form. Please take lots of notes as you work through this book.

Make notes of books you want to add to your reading list, products you want to try, services you want to check out, and so forth. Eventually, you need to sit down with the list of to-dos you've put together. Prioritize them and begin taking action!

Print out the Change Plan. Keep it close as you go through this book. Keep notes about things you might want to do, products you might want to try, and so forth. Determine which actions you need to take, and write them in your change plan.

For example, if you need to choose a PSA, actions might include signing up for trials with SolarWinds MSP, ConnectWise, SyncroMSP, and Autotask.

Later, you'll prioritize all the actions you've decided to take. And, of course, you then need to execute the highest priority actions you've identified.

Opportunity Everywhere!

> *"The future is already here.*
>
> *It's just not widely distributed."*
>
> *-- William Gibson*

I love this quote.

It is very true with regard to so much technology today – especially cloud services. The cloud is already here but lots and lots of people don't know about it. Much of what we talk about here is almost unchanged since we started selling it in 2008. So some people have had this for eleven years.

And others haven't started looking yet.

Another favorite quote is:

> *"The factory of the future will have only two employees, a man and a dog.*
>
> *The man will be there to feed the dog.*
>
> *The dog will be there to keep the man from touching the equipment."*
>
> *-- Warren Bennis*

We are getting close to this with robotics and driverless cars.

My daughter is in her mid-twenties. Her children will never learn to drive a car. I probably own the last car I'm going to own. My current car will be ten years old in 2025. Between driverless cars, Uber, and Lyft, why would I invest in another? I can rent a car when I go someplace or there'll be an app and a car will magically show up.

We are in an era where things are moving very fast and there's a dizzying amount of change. For example, look at all the light bulbs in an average office building or hotel. All of those lights are going to be replaced with smart LEDs. Soon.

And as TCP/IP becomes dominant in security, lighting, signage, business machines, and everything else, *you will have more opportunity in the next 10 years than the last 50 years*. It is a truly great time to be in a technology business!

But you can't think of it in terms of *servers*. Servers are not the answer. They probably haven't been for a while, but again, that knowledge isn't widely distributed.

There will always be a need for certain older technologies, but right now your opportunities are exploding. Think about IoT – the Internet of Things. Very soon, every light bulb in most office buildings will have an address and need to be monitored. Does that fit in your business model? It should!

Even the way we monitor security for IoT will be different. We won't look at each individual bulb and say, "Oh, this bulb at that address is throwing an alert." That would be impossible with tens of thousands (or hundreds of thousands) of devices. We're going to be looking at the entire pattern of all the traffic and then seeing when something is different. Then engineers can identify a problem. It's not because the memory on the server reached X%: It's because a pattern emerged that isn't recognized in the flow of data.

If you expand your knowledge and skillset to LED and other new technologies, your opportunities will explode.

The good news is that every one of those kinds of technologies is moving toward TCP/IP. So anyone who wants to move to the newer technologies will have to hire network engineers to get to the next level. (I assume TCP/IP means IPv6. Newer technicians will assume that. Older techs better get used to it.)

As a technology consultant, you have to step up and learn new technologies. If you don't, the opposition will hire network engineers and learn your technology. You have the advantage because you already master the networking protocols. But you can't rest on that. You need to keep learning.

In my opinion, it's all about opportunity, and I don't think we have any threats going forward. I really believe that everybody reading this book has an explosion of opportunities, and you have to decide what you're going to focus on to make money in the next few years. Someone is going to master the new technologies and make a lot of money. It's yours if you want it.

What is The Cloud? What is Not The Cloud?

So, what constitutes "The cloud?"

Nicholas Carr wrote a great book called *The Big Switch*. He talks about the evolution of electricity and how it's analogous to the evolution of the cloud. There was a time when, if you wanted electricity, you had to generate your own.

If you were on a farm, you had to have a windmill or you had to be near a river so that you could turn a water wheel and generate electricity to run your equipment. If you were in the big city, you wanted to be within the three-block area where Edison could get power to your building, or you had a power station in the basement.

Over time, technology evolved to have centralized ways that you could buy electricity and then the generators just moved somewhere else. With the distribution of AC (alternating current), electricity could be generated hundreds of miles away.

Today, we plug something into the wall and electricity is just there. We pay for it as we need it, turn it on when we need it, turn it off when we don't need it.

The Internet became the same way. And, he argues, the cloud became the same way. It used to be that if you wanted storage, you bought a storage device. And if you wanted computing capacity, you bought a server and you bought processors. But we've evolved from there.

My favorite example of something moving to the cloud is voicemail. Voicemail used to be an answering machine that was huge, and it had a reel-to-reel tape. Then the machine got smaller and smaller, and the tape got smaller and smaller. Eventually, the tape disappeared and it was digital. Then voicemail was built into the phone; and then it became built into the wall and the phone company sold you voicemail.

Today you have voicemail on every phone number. You probably have voicemail boxes that you never answer or look at, or ever use, because it's just included with the phone service and you don't need it. But it's there all the time.

And here the best part: You don't know where your voicemail is stored. You don't know what server it's on, how big the hard drives are, how much memory it has, or whether it's even backed up.

You don't know whether it's on redundant systems. You might assume that you know what country it's in, but you don't really know that.

It's just voicemail. It's just there. It's just on. It just works.

That's what technology needs to become for all businesses. It's just there; it just works. NOT "It's in that rack that I have to air-condition."

You need to let the client stop worrying that hard drives will get too old and stop spinning. Technology needs to *just be there*, just be secure, and just work.

When you talk about cloud services, you are probably the only one that needs to know where that stuff actually is. Your clients don't need to know where it is. They don't care, as long as they look you in the eye and say, "I'm going to sign this piece of paper because I trust you. You're taking care of my network."

You have to do the due diligence to sell the right thing, but they don't really know or care where that stuff is. They just want it to work.

Consider the current epidemic of ransomware. Your clients just want to look at you and say, "Is it going to be okay? Did you take care of us before this happened so that we're either not affected or we're not as affected as we might otherwise be?"

You need to make good choices with email, cloud services, storage, backup, antivirus, spam filtering, and everything else that goes into a comprehensive offering.

Yes, it's true that "The Cloud" is just someone else's computer. But quite realistically, we need to take full advantage of fully hosted services and let that "someone else" worry about the servers.

For your clients, The Cloud is simply technology that works all the time, and that is purchased as a service. It allows them to reduce capital expenditures but requires them to increase operating expenses.

YOU have to make sure you sell the right thing. That means you have to verify that you've chosen good partners, that the services are secure, and that downtime is as low as humanly possible. As we'll talk about later in the book, you are also responsible for all the configurations and documentation. You need to make the client feel that it's "safe" to stop worrying and just enjoy using cloud services.

A Few Key Take-Aways:

- "The future is already here. It's just not widely distributed."
  – William Gibson

- You don't know (or care) where your voicemail is.

- Clients don't care about The Cloud. They just want their stuff to work.

Additional Resources to Explore

- *DotCom Secrets* by Russell Brunson. See also ClickFunnels. com

- *The Big Switch* by Nicholas Carr.

2. My Company's Move to the Cloud

Let me give you a little background on how I got to the cloud.

First, the "before" time – before I became a consultant. I was running a small company that sold online information to lobbyists, state agencies, and other information vendors. "Online" meant that the data sat on my servers and companies paid to have access to it.

We put information from state legislatures into big databases, and then people subscribed to our service. This was in the early 1990s, before commercial enterprises could access the Internet.

Clients dialed into our computers with phones and modems. In many cases, we rented them the modem coupler and terminal printers. I had a bank of 72 modems connected to an HP 3000, and they ran reports using our service.

When PCs came along, and Windows 3 was actually a usable operating system, clients could use terminal emulators to get into our service. Eventually, I hooked that system to the Internet in 1993. I actually had to write an essay making the case that we should be allowed to access the public Internet. (That requirement was eliminated in 1994.)

After that, I went to work at Hewlett Packard. I was Site Manager for PC Software support. That means I ran the internal tech support team for HP's Roseville, California plant. We managed about 5,000 desktops and about 7,000 machines altogether.

I had a team that ran the Unix (HP-UX) help desk. And I had a team that performed all the daily backups for all servers at the HP Roseville plant. At that time, the daily backup was done on DAT-

72 tapes. There were racks and racks of them, and there was a 365-day rotation. So when a backup was done, it was actually taken offsite for a year before those tapes could be used again.

At this point, I had experience with the HPE 3000, Unix, Novell, Windows, and NT Server. Eventually, I left HP and began consulting multiple clients at once.

My company grew, in large part because we embraced Microsoft technology just as Microsoft decided to embrace small business.

Buying Nicko's Company

Skip ahead a bit. By 2005 I had six employees and decided that we needed to move to the cloud. But we knew there were some intermediary steps. I didn't know we'd go through all those steps in a few months!

I bought another consulting company from my friend Nicko. He had done a lot of web hosting, all on his own servers. So now we moved into a new office and we literally had a rack of my servers and a rack of his servers.

We turned a 6' by 10' storage area into the server room. We finished the walls, put in an air-conditioner, and installed a bunch of 30-amp dedicated circuits. And we put a lock on the door.

This was a very nice setup. We had the blue network (blue CAT-5 cables) and the green network (green CAT-5 cables) to distinguish web servers from the machines that ran our internal business. It was awesome.

Until a couple of months later.

The guy in the next office building decided that there couldn't be anything underneath his parking lot because it had been there *forever*. So he dug a hole in the parking lot, cut through an electrical cable, and blew out a transformer that was right outside our building. This was one of those big four-foot cubes. It took out all the electricity for several blocks around for four days.

All of my servers were offline. I literally had to go down to Home Depot, buy a generator, and have a big cable made so I could run the generator outside but plug in all my servers inside. Then I had to pay somebody to sit outside so nobody would steal the generator.

I couldn't lock the door because this big cable was in the way. I had to plug my UPS's into the generator, not knowing whether they were rated for use with a generator. But it didn't matter. I had no choice. And when it was all over I had to buy all-new UPS's anyway.

And that's the day I decided, "We're not doing this again. This will never happen again."

We rented space in a network colocation facility with literally unlimited bandwidth. Between the cost of electricity and the cost of air-conditioning, we saved enough money to pay for our colocation facility. Then, I started moving all those websites to hosted cloud services (or fired some clients for other reasons).

It was also a good opportunity to weed out some clients that didn't fit our model going forward.

Anyway, we moved people off our systems or up to the cloud one client web site at a time. This freed up our racks to put some of our clients' machines there and to back up our clients' machines to us. Overall, it was very handy to have the data center facility.

Eventually, we moved more and more systems to the cloud – including our own. It got down to us having one server, and all it did was provide Active Directory and store our QuickBooks. (You probably know that QuickBooks does not perform well over the Internet.)

We eventually put that last server in the colo. We ran Foundation Server 2008 because it was the last version that allowed a domain controller and remote access on the same machine. We had a three-user license for QuickBooks, and we remoted into that machine to manage our books.

That's basically the setup we had until 2017 when I finally moved to QuickBooks Online.

Bottom Line: Living in the Cloud with Managed Service

So, our data has been stored in the cloud as primary storage since 2008. We copy it back down to a physical drive as a backup. Live data are in the cloud; backup is on a physical drive in our office.

KPEnterprises grew to be about twelve people, plus the occasional intern or temp. Eventually, I sold that business to my service manager Mike. A couple of years later he sold it again. While Mike owned it, I sat at my old desk, did the same thing, did the sales, managed some migration projects, and did a lot of the customer-facing management.

When he sold the business again, I started another IT business and ran that for a few years. Finally, around December 2016/January 2017 I sold that as well. I still work with Tom, the guy who bought the business. He brings me in for certain projects and client meetings.

As you can see, I have lots of experience with lots of different technology and different business models. I am not so committed to one technology or one business model that I can't keep looking for something better.

My march to "managed service" really began around 1999 when I decided that we needed to make systems as reliable and as reasonably priced as possible. I started working to develop "flat fee" maintenance programs. It was a form of managed services, but we didn't have that name yet. I wanted to have a flat fee that was as predictable as possible for clients and as profitable as possible for us.

Profitability has always been a big driver for me. As a result, I'm not going to ever be tied to a technology just because I know it really well and I can make a bunch of money on it. Probably the one product I made more money on than anything else was Small Business Server. Between 2003 and 2008, we just took money to the bank in wheelbarrows selling that product.

But I'm not going to try to replace it or replicate it in any way. Its era has passed, and I just need to do whatever makes sense going forward.

Computers in Small Business

Computers haven't been used in small business for very long. In the 1970s and 1980s, small businesses either bought time on mainframe computers or invested in "mini" computers such as the IBM AS/400 or HP 3000.

A great example of renting time on mainframes was the old process of counting votes on election night. Many cities and counties used punch card ballots, but they had no way to tally them. So they took the ballots to someone's mainframe system. I happen to know that, in Spokane, Washington, this was the local electrical utility.

The owner of the mainframe rented time on the system to read the punch cards and tally the election results. It made no sense, at the time, for the county elections office to buy a half-million dollar computer just to count votes. So they bought time on an existing system.

Remember this distinction when someone says that going forward into the cloud is the same as going backward to the world of terminals and time sharing.

A few early home computers made their way into businesses, but it took Windows 3.0 to make the microcomputer a standard. And today's PC (the most common device in a business, whether it's a laptop or a desktop) is going to be a piece of the puzzle for a long time.

Some may ask about VDI or Virtual Desktops. Virtual desktops have a tough time in smaller markets because it's hard to justify the cost when the device that you use to access it has enough power to run Word, Excel, PowerPoint, and Outlook. That's most of what most people need.

So much for the desktop. The late 1990s and early 2000s saw a similar evolution to putting servers in offices. The most successful early servers were Novell. Then Microsoft jumped into the game.

With servers, offices could suddenly have centralized file storage (and sharing). They could secure data and Internet access. They could even have their own email system and databases, so they didn't have to rely on anyone for those services.

Just as early electrical users had to generate their own electricity, so did a generation of businesses generate their own computing power. We (IT consultants) brought lots of great technology into small businesses because we brought them their own Exchange Server, their own SQL Server, their own file server, their own backup system. And with SBS (Microsoft Small Business Server), we brought it all in one big box.

Today very few of us would choose to install an Exchange Server on site for a small office. But fifteen years ago we happily did it with offices of five or ten!

You would be amazed at how many problems go away when Exchange is not in-house. Of course it's just a simpler environment. And even though Exchange basically never breaks, lots of tickets go away once it's gone.

Now we're moving to the cloud. The backup is in the cloud. Email's in the cloud. Storage is in the cloud. SQL is in the cloud. And most new businesses would never consider buying a server.

If you were fresh out of high school or college, I don't think you'd go into the business of installing servers into small and medium businesses. No. You'd be selling them cloud services.

That's what you should be doing today – and from now on.

Managed Services and My Move to the Cloud

When I first started using modern tools for managed services (RMM and PSA), the only products that were really ready for prime time were Kaseya and ConnectWise.

Kaseya does lots of things, but is fundamentally a Remote Monitoring and Management (RMM) system. It was pretty expensive, but I saved enough money via my ASCII membership to pay for my ASCII membership for years. Kaseya required that we have our own SQL Server, and it needed a dedicated server. So we had that hardware and software expense on top of the Kaseya licenses.

ConnectWise is a Professional Services Automation (PSA) system. I bought it to run my company, manage billing, track tickets, and manage employees. Like Kaseya, it required that we have our own SQL Server, and it needed to be a dedicated server. So we had that hardware and software expense on top of the ConnectWise licenses.

Skip ahead four years. We highly recommend that everyone replace servers every three years. We had to decide what to do with these two dedicated servers. Note: we were also running our own Small Business Server in-house.

Now I was looking at a very big expense to replace two servers and commit to the licensing for another three or four years. Neither Kaseya nor ConnectWise had a cloud-based solution at the time.

So, we moved to Continuum (Zenith Infotech at the time) for the RMM, which was totally cloud-based. We didn't need any specific equipment to make it work – just a web browser. And we moved to Autotask for the PSA. Again, it was totally based in the cloud so we didn't have to get a server for that either.

Note: It's not the easiest thing in the world to move from one PSA or one RMM to another, but it is entirely possible. And it didn't kill us. So I guess it made us stronger.

All that transition was taking place right as my neighbor cut the cable and started us down the very quick path to the colocation facility. Once we had the colo, some very cool new options opened up for us.

At the time of the 2008-2010 (more or less) recession, we had a small vertical market in companies that worked with the housing industry. We had a custom lumber mill, we had a sod farm, we had a construction engineer, and we had a few folks that did marketing for new home developments.

These folks were not necessarily destroyed by the recession, but they were in a lot of pain.

One day, one of our favorite clients, Debbie, called. She said that they were bleeding money and had to make major cuts. She had already laid off a few people. And, she said, "You need to help us save money."

Her idea was that she could somehow reduce the amount of technology they had and therefore reduce the cost of maintaining it. My brother Manuel was president of my company at the time. He started a *business-focused* discussion with her.

Debbie revealed that their lease was almost up on their office, and their big phone system. So she was planning to move to a smaller office and get a smaller phone system.

Manuel then pitched an idea for a virtual office. Because we now had space in a data center, he told Debbie that she could save a lot of money by not paying rent on an expensive office in the Bay Area. He told her we'd take care of her server and we'll put it in our colocation facility. Then someday it'll become virtualized, and someday it will simply cease to exist.

And he told her, "You won't care and you won't know the difference. You won't have downtime, and we're going to take care of your data." He told her to send her employees home and we'll make sure they're taken care of.

Note: At no point did we promise to cut the amount she paid us. After all, we were saving her lots of money on rent. Plus, we set them up with a hosted phone system, and unplugged their old one.

As Manuel will tell you, Debbie said yes to this idea right away, largely due to her long relationship with our company and the fact that we had been taking care of her technology for thirteen years.

Eventually, Debbie actually moved to Connecticut and all her employees stayed in California. And everything just kept working. As promised, her machine was eventually retired and all her data and email moved to hosted cloud services.

So that's our story. In very short order, we moved our company to the cloud and started moving our clients to the cloud. We designed our first Cloud Five-Pack™ and started selling it as our primary offer. And it's been going gangbusters ever since.

I'm sure you're familiar with the concept of managed services. Well, a lot of people call themselves Managed Service Providers (MSPs) as a term that replaces the whole concept of outsourced IT or computer consultant.

In my mind, managed service means you actually take some ownership in the network. It means that you are responsible for that network. It means you maintain networks and prevent problems.

Offer Managed Services with Cloud Services – But Avoid All You Can Eat!

One goal of managed service is to flatten the IT spending as much as possible. That does NOT mean "all you can eat." Never use the term "all you can eat" because what a client can eat is your entire business. So just avoid that.

A consultant emailed me a couple of years ago and asked if he could have a call and talk about a problem. I said, "Sure." He was in trouble because he signed an all-you-can-eat contract. One of his customers went out and bought a bunch of Windows 8 machines that were eligible to be upgraded for free to Windows 10.

They did not buy the machines from him, but they called him and said, "You're supposed to give us all the labor for free, so we need you to come in and upgrade these machines to Windows 10 for free – before the free upgrade expires." He was (understandably) freaking out.

He said, "I don't know how I'm going to do this. It's going to cost me thousands of dollars of labor and I can't charge them for it." I told him, "Either you have to do it or you have to break the contract. Those are really your choices here. But whatever you do going forward, never sign anything else that ever says 'all you can eat.' That is not what managed services is about."

Memorize this:

Managed Service covers the maintenance of the operating system and software.

Under this definition, there's a portion of your labor that constitutes maintenance, which is covered under an MSA (managed service agreement). So, if you are making sure that something continues to work, that's included. If it's an add/move/change, it is *not* included and you're going to bill for that labor.

That's a nice black line that we draw between billable and unbillable. For example, if you ask me to install Photoshop on a machine, that's an add/move/change, that is a billable task. As soon as Photoshop is up and working, then if anything breaks we will fix it for no additional charge because that's maintenance.

That description is one that clients understand and employees understand. It makes a lot of sense, and helps people understand the line between maintenance and add/move/change.

Another component of managed services is also relevant to the discussion of cloud services and licensing. There's a method of buying and deploying licenses I call "managed service pricing." It is a tiered pricing structure based on the total number of licenses you've deployed, as compared to just the number installed at a single office.

For example: Let's look at selling antivirus into an office with 27 employees. In the old days, we would sell them one five-pack and one 2Five-pack™ of AV licenses. There are three unused licenses, but no one cares because it was the cheapest way to buy 27 licenses.

Now we don't do that. Now we buy and deploy exactly as many licenses as we need. Our pricing level is not based on five-packs or 2Five-pack™s but on the total licenses deployed across all clients. So you might get a price break at 1,000 licenses and 10,000 licenses deployed overall.

And that was a key to the evolution of the Cloud Five-Pack™ because, as you'll see soon, the five-pack we sell almost always has unused licenses. In this same scenario, I'm selling six Cloud Five-Packs™. There are still three unused licenses. But now, my company gets to keep the money for the unused licenses.

Remember: 80% of your clients will have unused licenses. I can already hear an objection ringing in your ears. Don't worry: I'll address that soon.

And finally, the last major component that makes this the perfect time to be selling cloud services: The **cost** of what you buy and sell is unrelated to the **price** that you sell it for.

Never – ever – think in terms of "margins" when you price cloud services. If you buy an RMM tool for $1.50 per device, for example, do not mark it up 3% or 10% or 20%. Don't even mark it up 50%. *Bundle it* into a bunch of offerings and sell it for $100 or $500.

Stop thinking in terms of the margin. I think the people who have gone down the wrong path in pricing are the ones who are selling everything on a cafeteria plan and they've got these tiny little margins all over the place. As a result, their clients are annoyed because they feel nickel-and-dimed to death – and the MSP isn't making real money.

What you pay and what you charge are unrelated to each other. And, again, managed service pricing makes it easier for us to bundle. You buy things in bulk, but all those components (email, antivirus, spam filtering, etc.) just become part of the "cost of production" for your overall cloud offering.

You can bundle up all your services and sell them in whatever service combination makes sense for you. I've always been a huge fan of bundles. Bundling services together makes a gargantuan difference.

A Few Key Take-Aways:

1. Why did in-house servers make sense in 2003 but don't make sense today? _____

    _____

2. Managed services covers maintenance of the operating system and software. (At least that's Karl's definition.)

3. Margin is irrelevant; cloud services should be priced on the value to the client, not the cost of delivery.

3. Cloud Computing in the Small Business Space

After several years of using the terms "cloud services" and "cloud computing" we still don't have a nice clear line we can draw to define what these are. It would be nice to check a box and say either *Cloud* or *Not Cloud*.

My local (regional) phone company sells old terminal server access to machines in their colocation facility and calls it cloud services. Does that mean anyone who's used RDP (remote desktop protocol) or RWA (remote web access) can say we've been doing cloud services since the year 2000, or even 1995?

Extremes like that make it hard to have a substantive discussion about cloud offerings. You need a clearer definition so you can determine how this fits with your business. It's not just a sales game.

I see four kinds of clouds, each of which provides its own opportunities for you:

1. Cloud-based services

2. Hosted servers

3. Hosted services

4. Hybrid cloud offerings

1. Cloud-based services are those that exist entirely in the cloud. You might use Salesforce.com or QuickBooks Online. Both of those are cloud-based services. Most "hosted" spam filtering is really a cloud-based service.

Your opportunities with cloud-based services can take many forms. The most common are reselling a service, acting as an affiliate for a service, or using a service as a component in one of your offerings.

If you resell a cloud-based service, it's usually the case that you buy at wholesale and sell at retail. For example, I might buy spam filtering for $2 per user and sell at $5 per user. The client relationship is with me. The service provider only knows enough about the client to provide the service. That usually does not include name, address, or financial information.

If you are an affiliate for the service, you make the sale, but the client gives their credit card to the service provider. You get paid a sales commission or referral fee of some sort. For example, you might sell a hosted voice over IP (VoIP) service. To conclude the sale, you simply manage the paperwork transaction between the client and the service provider. With luck, you get a percentage of their monthly payment every month.

There are two important factors to consider when you sell as an affiliate. First, you have to figure out which kind of payment you prefer. Some services give you a commission for as long as the client is their customer.

So, for example, if that phone service client is no longer one of your managed service clients, you'll still receive commission payments for as long as they have that phone service. Remember Debbie from the last chapter? She still pays her phone bill every month. And I get a commission check after more than ten years.

Some services give affiliates a one-time payment. So, you might earn a (much larger) commission at the beginning and then you're done. After that, the service gets to keep 100% of the monthly payments. Some services let you choose whether you want to be a reseller or an affiliate.

The second important factor to consider when you are deciding what you want to sell is the question of client ownership: Who "owns" the client? In other words, is this *your* client or the phone company's client? The way I see it, the client belongs to whoever charges the client's credit card every month.

In the spam filtering example, the client may or may not know who the service provider is. Even if they see the brand name, they know that they make their monthly payment to you. You own that client. You can switch them to an alternate provider very easily.

In the case of the VoIP provider, they own the client. They ding the credit card. They can switch the "agent" relationship to someone other than me. That means, if I'm not the agent of record, my monthly payments would stop. The client may or may not remember who sold them this service because the provider bills them every month.

The final way you can make money with cloud-based services is to roll them into your own branded offering. This is the most common option for most services. For example, our Cloud Five-Pack™ includes disc storage in the cloud, Exchange mailboxes, spam filtering, antivirus, and RMM (remote monitoring and management).

In this case, the spam filtering is just one ingredient in the bundle. This brings us back to the earlier discussion about the "managed service model" for pricing. You buy spam filtering per user or per mailbox. Because you buy in bulk, you get a good price. And rather than selling the services individually, you are selling them as part of your bundle.

2. Hosted Servers

Here's a technology that's been around for decades and now we can put a cloud label on it! Hosted servers are exactly that: Somewhere (out on "the cloud") there's a machine, or a virtual machine, running your operating system and application. For example, you can pay monthly for a hosted Windows Server on Amazon, Azure,

Rackspace, or 10,000 other places. You mark up this service and sell it to your client.

What you are selling is access to a complete server. That Windows Server might be running Exchange Server. In such a case, you would manage this Exchange Server just like a physical server that lives in your office.

Important note: When you sell hosted servers, those servers need the same maintenance as a physical server. That means they need to be monitored, patched, and backed up. The provider won't do anything for you. YOU are the tech support for these servers. This is important because you need to charge for that maintenance as well as for the services themselves.

In my opinion, such hosted servers cannot be included in the category we call *serverless technology* – because there's a server you need to maintain.

3. Hosted Services

Hosted services are different altogether. Hosted services may exist on a physical machine or a virtual machine somewhere, but you can't access the machine – only the service you are buying or reselling. What you buy is a small piece of what that machine is *doing*. A perfect example of this is a hosted Exchange mailbox.

Hosted Exchange mailboxes are instances of Exchange running on an Exchange Enterprise Edition server. The company that owns that Exchange server has to maintain it. They have to keep it patched and fixed and updated. They have to fix anything that breaks.

You literally sell (resell) access to one mailbox at a time. If something goes wrong, you really can't fix it. All you can do is to contact the provider and ask them to fix their stuff. You might pay $8 per month for a mailbox and sell it for $15. You do not have to charge a maintenance fee because you have no maintenance costs.

Generally speaking, each service has a cut-over threshold that makes it more rational to choose either a hosted server or hosted services. Hosted services work great for small to medium size clients while hosted servers make sense for larger clients. Consider ten user mailboxes at $15 each vs. 100 mailboxes at $15 each. At some point the individual mailbox cost exceeds the cost of a hosted server running Exchange Server.

4. Hybrid Cloud Offerings

Hybrid clouds are essentially cloud services with some components on site. One example of this is Zynstra's Hybrid Cloud Server. It is sold, for example, as an HPE Proliant box at the client's office on which you run virtual machines. The box controls all licensing and monthly charges via a hosted service. See https://www.zynstra. com/proliant-easy-connect/.

Another hybrid cloud example could be something you create yourself by combining on site components with cloud components. Let's say you charge the client $100 a month to have 250 GB of "storage" that's always backed up and instantly available.

This might include a small server on site for fast access, which is backed up in real time to a cloud service (see the upcoming "Server Lite" discussion). In such a setup, the client pays you a service fee, you own the hardware, and the cloud storage component is just a piece of the cloud storage you buy and resell each month.

No matter which combination of these four kinds of cloud offerings you choose to sell, there's plenty of money to be made in cloud services. More and more we're becoming comfortable with services that we don't own, we don't control, and we don't maintain.

If you're new to the business, cloud-based tools and offerings are all you've ever known. If you've been in business for more than a few years, you have adopted cloud technologies and woven them into your business offerings.

The easiest and most obvious cloud offerings are (more or less in order):

- Hosted spam filtering

- Cloud-based backup and disaster recovery

- Cloud-based storage

- Hosted line of business (LOB) applications

- Hosted services (e.g., buying hosted Exchange services one mailbox at a time)

- Hosted servers on a platform such as Azure or Amazon Web Services

Less obvious services include hosted intrusion detection, content filtering, antivirus, and mobile device management. These are services you can easily provide to your clients and fit into the managed services pricing model.

With the implementation of 5G wireless over the next few years, we will see routers and firewalls disappear into the cloud. We are at the delightful convergence of massive bandwidth and massive compute capacity growth.

One More Cloud Product

There's another kind of cloud service you might be involved with that I do not consider to be one of the four clouds: A cloud-based development environment. I mention it here but not later in the book because it is really a product (application) development platform and not a piece of a managed service business.

Microsoft's Azure (www.windowsazure.com) offers a cloud-based development environment. Microsoft has developed several tools for creating applications and web sites that exist only within the Azure environment. So, for example, you can manage a SQL "instance" without having to manage the server it's running on.

You may not be a developer today. But programming against the Azure cloud is not difficult. And you can always hire someone on an hourly or project basis to develop applications. See UpWork (upwork.com), formerly odesk.com and elance.com.

The Small Business Bias

As these cloud offerings (and even managed services themselves) become more powerful, more commonplace, and easier to install and support, we see many very big businesses trying to sell into our space. One of the constant discussions at SMB conferences is "Should I be worried about [Dell] [Office Depot] [Staples] [Best Buy] [Ingram Micro] [etc.] selling directly to my clients?"

For the most part, I say no. There are two reasons for this. First, we have been concerned about this for fifteen years and have never actually seen it happen. Second, and most importantly, small businesses like doing business with small businesses. They want to call you personally. They don't want a support line in another country. They don't want to be on hold.

In fact, your clients could have moved themselves to Small Business Server with Internet access fifteen years ago. When you think in those terms, they've never "needed" you. But they want you. They don't know any more about choosing the right cloud services than they knew about picking the right server hardware.

. . . And now someone in the crowd needs to mention that they make a lot of money and get a lot of new clients by fixing home-grown network projects. Well, guess what? You're going to make a lot of money and get new clients from fixing home-grown cloud projects.

At the end of the day, businesses are most comfortable doing business with companies their own size. We actually have a client who has told us that he never wants his data or servers touched by anyone he hasn't met and looked in the eye. So he might put a backup in our colo, but he's never going to back up to an unknown cloud in an unknown location.

Even when these clients buy services from big providers such as Rackspace or Amazon, they don't ever want to deal with Rackspace or Amazon. They want to call you. They will only call you.

In my last real job before I became a consultant, we were migrating a massive three-state operation from mini computers (HP 3000s) with dumb terminals to NT servers with SQL and PCs on the desktop. The big buzzwords then were "Client Server." Are you using client-server technology? Is this a client-server application?

The transition to client-server was little more than a label we could use to describe what we were already doing. We had long ago moved away from dumb terminals. We had maybe 25 dumb terminals in the office and 25 workstations with terminal emulator programs. We had computing power on the desktop, so creating a system that took advantage of that fact was an obvious next step. Our NT/SQL combination required a client component.

Cloud computing is similar. It's the obvious next evolution in technology. Many of us had been inching into it for years before it had a label. For example, on-premises spam filtering used to be a real option. Now it has all but disappeared (at least in the small business space). Hosted spam filtering just makes sense. You may have inherited an on-premises spam filter in the last five years, but I bet you haven't sold a lot.

The Bottom Line on Cloud Services

Cloud services are here to stay. Some of them are a new label on older practices. Many are truly new and powerful options. For example, I hate on-premises line-of-business (LOB) applications for the most part and love hosted LOBs. Many on-premises LOBs have been a pain to support and expensive to upgrade. Hosted LOBs are always up to date and fit into that pricing model we discussed before: The client pays for what they use and generates monthly recurring revenue.

Many people have been selling managed services as an on site only service. We're going to discuss how you can easily integrate cloud services into your managed services model. One of my old promises is that I would try to keep adding services to my managed service and cloud service offering so that we provide more to the client for the same price. We'll show you how easy that is.

Remember, whether you're talking about pure-cloud offerings, hosted servers, or hosted services, you have many options. In fact, you have an almost unlimited number of options.

You can get hosted "office" products from Google as well as Microsoft. You can put Linux servers at Microsoft and buy Windows Servers on Amazon. You can buy just plain processing power from Google, Microsoft, Nvidia, and others.

Just as you have selected your favorite flavors for desktops, laptops, and tablets, you'll be selecting your favorite flavors for cloud services as well.

(Side Note) Wait. I Thought Azure Was The Cloud

Microsoft would like you to believe that Cloud = Azure. Or Cloud = Office 365 (O365). In fact, they've attempted to appropriate the term "Cloud Service Provider" (CSP) as someone who sells their cloud services.

I have developed products and services on Azure. I believe they have their place. I believe they are among the best cloud services you can resell. But your long-term success depends on you selling the right tool for the job. Here are the weaknesses of Azure as your sole solution for cloud services.

First, a lot of what you want to sell isn't available on Azure. The Microsoft options for antivirus and spam filtering are limited. Their options for storage may be right for some people but not for everybody. And so, if you want to put together a killer bundle of cloud services, it might not be possible to stick to an all-Microsoft answer.

Second, most of the services people point to on Azure fall into the category of *hosted servers*, not *hosted services*. If you stick with hosted servers, you will be doing the maintenance on those servers. In addition to that, you'll be back to installing Exchange servers and SQL servers for a handful of users.

Hosted services such as hosted Exchange mailboxes through O365 are a great piece of your cloud offering. You just have to decide whether you want to sell directly through Microsoft and their interface or sell through a reseller or distributor. (Don't worry, we'll come back to this discussion.)

Other solutions, such as mapped drives to cloud storage with file versioning and backup, can be accomplished with Azure resources. But to stick to a strictly-Microsoft solution, you would have to do a lot of scripting. Again, there's nothing wrong with that. But I'm a big fan of reselling solutions that someone has already built . . . and I like to rely on them to do the support.

If I build a massive collection of "solutions" based on scripts that only my employees and my company use, then I am tied into doing one hundred percent of the support when something goes wrong. And "goes wrong" can be as simple as Microsoft releasing an update or script version.

My approach – my bias – is very strongly in favor of reselling services for a markup. I believe this is the future of cloud services in small business. It's tried, it's tested, and it's proven.

The future is here . . .

A Few Key Take-Aways:

1. The four primary types of cloud services are:

    a. Cloud-based services

    b. Hosted servers

    c. Hosted services

    d. Hybrid cloud offerings

2. Hosted servers require about the same amount of maintenance as a physical server at a client office.

3. Hosted services require no maintenance on your part.

4. You should not worry about large corporations selling services into your small business client base. Your clients prefer to work with companies your size.

Additional Resources to Explore

*   Upwork – www.upwork.com

*   Microsoft's Azure – www.windowsazure.com

*   QuickBooks Online – www.quickbooksonline.com

*   Salesforce.com – www.salesforce.com

*   Zynstra – www.zynstra.com/proliant-easy-connect

II. Right Sizing Your Offering

4. One Size Does Not Fit All

When we first started deploying servers into small businesses, there was really only one "size" of operating system. You either installed Novell or Unix, and later Windows NT or Linux. So when I say there was only one size of O.S., it was kind of a one-size-fits-all world.

Hardware was much more variable. On the low end, some clients deployed what you and I would call desktop hardware, but put a server operating system on it. After all, the hardware didn't know what you were installing.

Eventually, true "server" hardware emerged. It had RAID controllers, could take multiple processors, and accepted a lot more RAM.

And while you can buy "servers" that are not very powerful, there are features that separate a real server from a wanna be server.

One of the reasons SBS (Small Business Server) had a great fifteen-year run is that it did an amazing amount of work if you installed it on the right box. While there have always been low-end servers, a great business class server would run SBS flawlessly despite the fact that we asked it to do a lot of work.

But just as SBS was getting the power it needed (running 64-bit and using more than four gigabytes of RAM), a lot of services were moving off to the cloud.

What's the right size server today? Well, that depends a great deal on who the customer is. If someone has 1,000 employees, then I think almost everyone reading this would say that we'll install some Exchange servers on site (or in the cloud). It makes sense for the workload – and that company is almost guaranteed to have an I.T. staff in-house to manage the servers.

On the other end of the scale, there are a lot of companies with fewer than twenty employees. According to the Small Business and Entrepreneurship Council, about 90% of all companies in the U.S. have fewer than twenty employees. (See http://sbecouncil. org/about-us/facts-and-data/.)

Today, there's no way I would deploy an Exchange server for 5, 10, 15, or even 20 people. Those days are gone. On site or in the cloud, that is simply the "old" way of doing business.

Aside from the cost of hardware, software, licenses, and electricity, on site servers are less secure and have more downtime than cloud-based services. Whether you buy direct from Microsoft or go through a reseller, a cloud-based hosted Exchange mailbox will have essentially zero downtime. And you will need to provide zero maintenance of whatever server it's on.

The Middle

Most of us support a number of clients in the big middle – Between twenty-one and 999 employees. And, truth be told, I think most people reading this primarily serve clients with 250 or fewer users.

So what should we sell them? At the low end, I think it's clearly hosted Exchange mailboxes. At the high end, it's still Exchange on site or Exchange servers in the Cloud. And even there, the on site option makes less sense every day.

But this is a changing landscape. And even if you finish this book and have a rock-solid cloud service offering that works today, you need to keep evaluating what's out there.

I believe we will be putting more and more (larger and larger) companies on hosted options every year.

In the big picture, it's obvious that the next five years or so are going to represent a transition period of hybrid solutions. That means some services will naturally be migrated to various cloud solutions. But lots of things are going to continue to live on site. The most obvious on site technology will continue to be printers, switches, desktop PCs, and LOBs (line of business applications) that cannot be moved to the cloud.

Just remember: Don't hold back. Don't keep everything on site simply because you have one or two services that have to be on site. And while we're in the hybrid world, keep an eye out for the next solution that needs to be moved to the cloud.

I'm a huge proponent of encouraging clients to stick to a three year replacement plan for hardware. For desktops and laptops, this means replacing roughly one-third of their machines each year. In that way, everything is always under warranty and everything generally runs smoothly. It also means replacing a server after three years.

I bring this up because this natural flow of transitioning to new equipment meshes well with a gradual migration to hosted servers and hosted services.

In the end, it comes down to right-sizing the client's technology.

Start Planning

One of the wisest things our company did way back in 2005 is to start planning how we would move each of our clients to the cloud. For some, it seemed impossible. For others it seemed obvious.

We started putting things in place by moving the smallest and most "obvious" clients to cloud services. Next, we moved entire classes of service to the cloud. For example, we used to sell on site devices for spam filtering. Once we decided to move everyone to hosted spam filtering, we did this across all clients.

Remember: Time is your friend. Every year, equipment gets a little older and a little slower. When you have ongoing discussions with clients about this, they begin to see that changes have to happen.

I love the example of network speeds (which we'll dive into in the next chapter). There was a time when all desktop machines started showing up with gigabit network cards. Within three years, every desktop and laptop had a gigabit card.

But in most cases, the fastest card on the server was 100 MBps. And in many cases, the switch had only a few gigabit ports. So we went through a period where the slowest network card in the office was on the server!

Then the server got replaced. And the switch got replaced. Now, the network was dragged down by the CAT-5 wiring in the walls. Gigabit everywhere, but effective speeds of 300-400 MBps until the wires got replaced.

And we all know, those wires rarely got replaced. But it didn't matter too much because the speeds from the desktop to the server were *fast enough*. There was, effectively, no choke point until you got to the Internet.

That scenario played out again and again across many clients. But everyone reading this probably knows some exceptions to the rule.

I had a client in 1995 that set up a new set of workstations. He had fifteen programmers and set up twenty new workstations because he didn't know how fast he was going to grow. And we wired them all up with fiber to the desktop. In 1995!

Why? Well, they were programmers. And when they hit "compile," there was a pause. If the pause was five seconds, the programmers took a sip of coffee. If the pause was sixty seconds, they got up, stretched their legs, and wondered off to talk to someone.

That client needed speed because the total hourly cost for programmers was extremely high. High enough to be calculated in dollars per second!

[Just so you don't think this guy was a jerk, he wasn't. In fact, he was one of the nicest employers I've ever met. He bought the programmers pizza several times a week and let them use the network for multi-player games that lasted late into the night. On a network most gamers would have killed for in 1995.]

Let me tell you a seemingly unrelated story. We always ask a standard set of "Roadmap" questions when we onboard a new client. One of these, of course, is how much tolerance they have for downtime.

We all tend to assume that clients absolutely have to have zero downtime – because that's what we would want if it was our company. But when you actually ask them, you find out that some clients really don't care. On more than one occasion I've had clients tell me that they wouldn't want to be without email for more than a week. A week!

The point is: Everyone is different. Some businesses can go "off line" for hours at a time with very little effect on profitability. Others measure downtime by the second because it's so expensive.

In a perfect world, each of these clients would be willing to pay maintenance and service fees consistent with their needs. But we all know that's not the case.

Whatever your clients' needs, you need to do enough research about who they are and what they need to be able to offer them the right services. And you need to do enough research about the services out there to make sure you line up client needs with best-fit services.

The Future is Already Here . . .

I would like to implore you to work on a new mindset for the rest of this book: **Be open to doing everything differently than you did in the past**.

I really believe that you can see the future if you stop looking at the things we've taken for granted for many, many years.

- Networks require wires
- The cloud requires massive bandwidth
- It won't happen in your lifetime
- Routers are hardware devices that live on site
- Firewalls too

I gave a presentation for CompTIA shortly before writing this chapter. After seeing my slide deck, I got a note that said, "We really want to move away from the change-or-die messaging." Well, okay. I can water it down.

But here's the bottom line: The world is changing very, very fast. And if you want to make the most money, you need to change with it. You need to see new things, and new ways of operating, as opportunities. As you'll see later on, I really believe a huge swath of this industry is living in the past.

Building your own servers and installing them in client offices is a dead business model. It is the past. Not only should we not be putting servers in client offices, most people shouldn't be putting virtual servers in the cloud.

Serverless technology is no longer new. It's proven and it's moving fast.

You absolutely need to right-size your offering for clients. And you absolutely will be in a hybrid environment for at least five or ten more years (with some technology in the cloud and some on site).

But don't fool yourself into believing that the old model is alive or that it's the right solution for most clients.

Be open to doing things in new ways. With new technology. And new opportunities.

It's almost impossible for us to challenge our own assumptions because they are so fundamental to our beliefs that we can't distinguish between absolute fact and absolute assumption.

This book is filled with very common-sense advice and very practical examples of cloud service offerings that I know work.

But underlying all of this is knowledge that the very core of our business is flipping upside down right now. And we need to tune into this change. Only then can we take advantage of the next great opportunities.

In order to get started, you need to develop one or two core cloud service offerings. But to be hugely successful, you also need to be open to new technologies and integrate them into your offerings as quickly as possible.

Get started.

Right-size for today.

Right-size for each client.

Right-size for the future.

One variable we haven't tackled yet is bandwidth. In the next chapter, we'll look at on site assessments and bandwidth.

A Few Key Take-Aways:

1. The size of your clients matters. The smaller they are, the faster you need to move them to hosted cloud offerings.

2. Very large clients will probably continue to have on site servers for a long time.

3. In addition to the costs of deployment, on site servers are virtually guaranteed to have more downtime than hosted services.

Additional Resources to Explore

• Small Business and Entrepreneurship Council - http://sbecouncil.org/about-us/facts-and-data

Note:

_____

_____

_____

_____

_____

_____

_____

_____

5. Assessing Client Networks

One of the misunderstandings people have about cloud services is that you have to have massive bandwidth. You don't. Consider this example:

If you've got an Exchange server in-house and the Internet goes down for, say, sixty seconds, ten times a day (which is a rather unreliable Internet connection), you will probably never notice it. At least you won't notice the email traffic.

When the Internet is up, the traffic will flow into the Exchange server. When it's down, you're looking at Outlook. So you don't know that the Exchange Server is offline. You can see Outlook, you can see everything.

Even when the Internet blinks, you can open email, reply to email, delete email, access your calendar, and do *most* of what you need to do in Outlook. Now think about what happens when you move that Exchange Server to the cloud.

You still access it with Outlook. Even when the Internet blinks, you can open email, reply to email, delete email, access your calendar, and do *most* of what you need to do in Outlook.

With an on site Exchange server, email might get bounced when your Internet connection is down. Of course, if you have a hosted spam filter, then email will not bounce; it will be stored until the spam filter can see your server again.

With hosted Exchange server (or hosted Exchange mailboxes), senders will never receive a bounce message because email will also continue flowing in. It might not get to your desktop Outlook – but it *will* still be downloaded to your cell phone, and it will still be available via a web interface.

So, moving email to a hosted solution will be almost identical to having an Exchange server on site. The primary exception is that you will have improved up-time overall.

When some people think about "cloud computing," they automatically think about using RDP or a similar technology to open a remote session to a remote server or remote desktop. And if that's true, then you really do need extremely good, reliable bandwidth.

But if it's *not* what you're doing, then you don't require extraordinary Internet bandwidth or reliability. Think about what you (and your clients) have experienced with your cell phones: As you drive from one part of town to another, or go on an elevator, things just kind of don't work for a minute.

And then everything works fine again. Overall, it's a minor distraction. Your life is not horrible. You do not have a panic attack when you get to the bottom of the elevator.

Your connectivity, overall, is good. It does what you need it to do. Now consider how "wired" phones have changed over the last twenty years. It's very similar.

Back in the 1950s (and 60s, and 70s, and 80s, and 90s), telephones were hard wired. And they just worked. In fact, they worked more than 99.9999% of the time. Wired telephone may just be the single most reliable technology in the history of the human race.

Then we started moving to voice over IP. Which is still very reliable. It's probably around 99.99% uptime (that's about four minutes of downtime per month). And it's everywhere. Most people don't even know that VoIP is the de facto standard and that virtually all telephone communication is now less reliable than it was twenty years ago.

That's what the transition to cloud services will be for most people. There might be a pause in synchronizing email or files. You might actually have to take a quarter of a breath before your data appears. But that will be the new normal. And we don't need to maintain physical servers in our offices to have good, reliable technology.

Right-Sizing Solutions

Now, having said all that, there are some Internet connections that are just too slow to support certain solutions. You need to sell the right solution. And that might mean selling the client a faster, or more reliable Internet connection.

Be careful that you don't limit future technology decisions due to current bandwidth. It may be that you need to create long-term plans to gradually increase bandwidth in order to gradually move clients into the right technology. Just don't keep selling "last year's solution" because you still have last year's bandwidth.

No matter what some people say, there is no one right answer to the question of how much bandwidth a client needs. They need enough to do what they're doing today AND they need enough to do what they'll be doing tomorrow. But I can almost guarantee that they don't need enough for everyone in the office to have a dedicated connection to their own virtual server (or virtual desktop for that matter).

Second Internet Connections and Failover

Internet connectivity has been growing faster and more reliable for thirty years – before most people knew it existed. But there are times when the Internet fails – or at least parts fail. So having a failover connection is not a bad idea.

But this also depends on the client's needs. If a client's entire sales operation is down whenever the Internet is down, then a failover makes sense. If a client is mildly inconvenienced because they have to answer email on their smart phone for five minutes every three months, they are probably not willing to pay for the failover.

More and more, we are actually able to generate a hotspot from our cell phones when the Internet is less reliable than we'd like. And as more and more companies offer unlimited data plans, I think we'll see more of this.

Remember the lessons of Superstorm Sandy (Google that if you need details). Hurricane Sandy hit the U.S. Northeast in October 2012. It hit New York particularly badly. There were businesses without electricity or Internet for more than two weeks.

Millions of people were without services for a full week. Many also had no cell phone service. The cellular service with the fewest problems was Verizon. All the others were down.

Some businesses literally set up offices in New Jersey and other places where they could get electricity and Internet connectivity.

Everyone whose entire business was in the cloud had zero downtime. Everyone who had mission critical servers on site was down. Period. The lesson from Superstorm Sandy is: The cloud is reliable enough to bet your entire business on.

And that was almost a decade ago. Cloud services are faster and more reliable than ever.

It was also a great boon for companies that were installing BDR (backup and disaster recovery) systems that could spin up virtual servers in the cloud. Many of those servers were never brought back down to the local offices.

My "Ideal" Small Business Network with Cloud Services

Let's look at a very practical view of what you actually need for most clients. The diagram above represents my network right now. Other than one change we'll discuss, this has been my network since 2008.

Until 2017, I had a three-user license for QuickBooks on my server. That's so my far-flung staff and I could all connect remotely and access QuickBooks. In 2017 I committed to QuickBooks Online. It's more expensive, but frees us from having to maintain QuickBooks on the server.

At the time, one of my administrative assistants lived in Florida. I live in California. Now, one of my admins lives in the Bay Area. Another is in Sacramento, but she only comes to my office once or twice a week. And, of course, I travel a lot. So, we all work effectively in the cloud.

ABC Solutions (Florida) helps me with QuickBooks Online and banking. My graphics people are in New York and Sacramento. They never come into my office but they do need to access my data. I have a programmer in India, a programmer in the Philippines, and two web developers in Sacramento. They never come into my office.

On and on and on. I have lots of people who work with me and who need access to specific data, but they never need to come into my office.

Clapton is the current server. QuickBooks is not installed on it. All it does is provide Active Directory (via Server Essentials 2016) and it is the backup for the online storage. That's all it does. Period. Soon you'll see exactly how that works. And then we have desktops and printers and so forth.

There are things that you will never get rid of: You're always going to have some physical infrastructure in-house. Printing is a perfect example. I don't ever see a day when I'm going to push a button to print something and Amazon's going to deliver it by flying robot. I just don't see that being feasible.

It's possible, because that technology exists. But it's not widely distributed because it's stupid. More and more, there are things that we *could do* that we're just not *going* to do.

So: You're going to have printers. You're going to have wires in the wall. And for the next five or ten years, you're going to have a wireless device, a firewall, a switch, and a router. There's going to be equipment in-house. That's good, especially if you sell equipment.

Note: With 5G wireless and cloud-based networking infrastructure, we will soon start to see offices without firewalls and routers on site. These will be delivered as cloud-based services. Just as people are saying, "Why should I buy an Exchange Server when I can get email in the cloud?" they will soon be asking why they should pay one time for a firewall that goes obsolete when they can buy a service in the cloud.

Today, many services no longer have to exist at a client's office: storage, virtual servers, SQL, Exchange, and more. Eventually this list will include file servers, line of business applications, and databases for all your clients. All those things exist up in the cloud on various services. They are on all the time. They are completely reliable.

Everyone on my staff – and on my clients' staffs – can work from home, from the office, or from anywhere in the country or the world. Making that work is more dependent on Standard Operating Procedures than technology. The technology has been around quite a while now.

A Few Key Take-Aways:

1. Cloud services do not necessarily require massive bandwidth.

2. Superstorm Sandy settled the question about whether cloud services are reliable enough for business.

3. For at least five to ten years, we'll be moving more and more services from on-site to cloud services.

Additional Resources to Explore

- QuickBooks Online – www.quickbooksonline.com

- ABC Solutions – www.abcsolutionsfl.com

6. Placing the X

There are many variations on this old story. I first heard it from Brian Tracy. All the variations claim to be true. As far as I know, it's just a good illustrative story:

> There was a factory that had a pressure leak somewhere in their systems, and they could not find the cause. They called in one specialist after another. Finally, they called in a consultant who was renowned as the best engineer in his field.
>
> The consultant walked all over the factory and looked at every pipe. Then he took out a large red marker and placed an "X" on a valve. He told them, "Replace that valve and your problem will be solved."
>
> The factory replaced the valve and, sure enough, it fixed the problem. The factory manager was happy – until he got the bill. The consultant had billed him $10,000 for consulting.
>
> The manager told the consultant, "I can't pay $10,000 for consulting. I need more detail about what we got for our money." So the consultant sent a revised invoice that read

Placing X on valve	$1
Knowing where to place the X	$9,999
Total	$10,000

I love this story for several reasons. First, it shows the power of knowledge. As consultants, the ultimate thing we sell is our knowledge – not our skills.

Second, I have always believed that finding the chokepoint – the X – in a network describes a great deal of what we do. Think about the advice you give to speed up a system. If the chokepoint is memory, you add more memory. If it's processing power, you add processing power. If it's storage, you add storage.

Eventually, if you can get the client to go along with your advice, you keep moving the chokepoint until it's outside the network you control. That used to mean that we were pretty happy once the Internet was the chokepoint.

That meant we'd done everything we could with the servers, the workstations, the wiring, the switches, etc. In a perfect world, you design and build and tweak systems until the slowest piece of the operation is outside your control.

But things are different with Cloud Computing. Now, we can't shrug off that slow Internet. We can't say the problem's with Microsoft (or Amazon or Sherweb or Rackspace). Now we need to bring all those services into our sphere of influence and make sure everything works together in an optimal configuration.

Note: Don't forget that point when we get to the question of why clients can't do this for themselves. They can't because they don't have the knowledge and experience. They can never see the really big picture and understand all the "moving parts" that make a modern network operate at peak efficiency.

Putting Everything Where It Belongs

In some ways, building a network is analogous to building a computer. But it's a step beyond. When building a computer, there's generally one mother board, one network card, a specific quantity of memory and hard drives, etc. You basically figure out what to build, then you put the pieces together.

Networks are mostly like that, but with a lot more variables. Modern networks are designed to operate within a much larger network of networks. So you have to figure out the best ways to give just the right amount of access while protecting the security of everything.

And while the client may think of you as a "technician," your real job is to balance productivity, security, flexibility, innovation, and costs. You are a manager of their network.

As we move to cloud services, we take all that to another level once again. Standard network management includes building flexibility that allows the client to move to a different line of business application, or a new ISP, for example.

With cloud services, you have the flexibility to move to a hundred different kinds and flavors of cloud storage. It's very different from choosing between SATA and SSD. Now storage includes variables such as speed of access, archive vs. live data, long term vs. short term storage, version control, etc.

And most importantly, you need to build a collection of seemingly-unrelated services and make them all look seamless to the client. They all need to work together. They all need to be secure. The security can't get in the way of productivity.

It all has to be future-proof. And it all has to be done at a reasonable price.

Three lessons come out of all this:

1. The client really can't do this for themselves. The best they can hope for is to create a "good enough" collection of cloud services. Which won't really be good enough.

2. You have to think in terms of bundles. You cannot sell an unlimited number of cafeteria plan add-ons and maintain the overall integrity of your cloud service offering.

3. At the same time, your bundle needs to be flexible enough to keep evolving over time. Eighteen months from now, you'll probably be including something that doesn't exist today.

Going forward, then, your job is to figure out what all the pieces are and to make sure each one of them is in the right place for each client.

For example: Where should email go? Right now, for most small businesses, it should probably go into hosted Exchange servers or hosted Exchange mailboxes. Where should storage go? Again, for most small businesses, it should probably be in the cloud. But for some clients it really has to be on site – backed up to the cloud.

Your job as the architect and manager of this growing array of services is actually a lot more complicated than it's ever been. The designing, architecting, and strategy are more complex than they've ever been.

As we'll see later, the actual execution of these big, complicated plans is much easier than it's been for the last twenty years. But that just makes the role of "consulting" – placing the X – more important than ever.

Here's what your job looks like for the next five to ten years:

- Help each client to place each service (Active Directory, storage, email, antivirus, routing, etc.) exactly where it belongs today.

- Make everything work together optimally.

- Be ready, willing, and able to move any individual service to a more-optimal place when new technology emerges.

In essence, your never-ending job will be to constantly provide the absolute best package of services while also constantly implementing newer, better, more-optimal services as they emerge. Clients are not able to do that. They need to focus on whatever they do for a living.

Trunk-slamming amateurs are not going to do that. They don't have enough knowledge about the big, big picture to put together the optimal network for a given client.

Your biggest competitor is not the managed service provider across town trying to sign your clients. Your biggest competitor is the "good enough" network and "good enough" cloud services.

As Jim Collins reminds us, "Good is the enemy of Great."

In the next chapter we'll walk through an exercise to diagnose client networks and begin the "cloud" conversation. Then, in the next several chapters we'll explore building your cloud service bundle and figuring out what the required services look like. In the section after that we'll look at pricing schemes and finalizing your bundle(s).

In the meantime, start thinking about your career as a consultant. Begin committing to the inevitable future where you have the never-ending job of re-engineering and re-architecting every client network again and again . . . from now on.

The days of building a server, making no changes for three or four years, and then doing it all again are over. Your future is one of constant change. And constant vigilance, as security must be maintained in an ever-changing environment.

A Few Key Take-Aways:

1. The value in consulting is in your knowledge – not your skills. That also means you need to be a life-long learner.

2. Technology consulting from now on will be cloud consulting. It is bigger and more complex than it's ever been.

3. There's no rest for the consultant. You will bundle a variety of disparate services, but the optimal bundle will change again and again, forever.

4. The actual execution of these big, complicated plans is easier than it's ever been, but that just makes the role of "consulting" – placing the X – more important than ever.

Additional Resources to Explore

- Brian Tracy. *Focal Point* is an excellent book. But also go get every audio program you can find on Audible or anywhere else. Really great stuff.

- Jim Collins. *Good to Great*.

Note:

7. Money-Making Homework - Network Assessments

Assignment: Test Client Bandwidth

Here's a great project you can execute. It will give you and your clients a lot of insight into their future cloud options. And it will probably result in a number of opportunities for you to sell new equipment and services in the short-term.

In the downloads that accompany this book (see Preface for instructions), there's a Bandwidth Worksheet. Modify that as you see fit, and perform this series of quick measurements at your office. Then repeat for all client offices.

Speed Test Example:

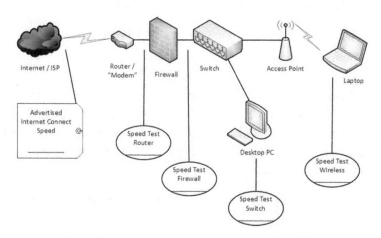

I highly recommend you create a service ticket for each client to measure bandwidth. Then select a preferred Speed Test tool, so that all of your technicians are using the same tool at each clients' office.

Right now, I guarantee you have clients whose networks are not as fast as they should be. And many will need faster networks once they start relying on cloud services. This project will give you great visibility about all client Internet operations.

Note: You'll have to decide whether this is billable work or included in your monthly service. It will probably take no more than 15-30 minutes on site at each client. Personally, we did not charge for this service because we knew it would lead to lots of additional work.

My Results

As of Spring 2019, the results for my office are as follows.

Advertised Internet Speed:	300 MBps
Speed inside router:	314 MBps
Speed inside firewall:	306 MBps
Desktop (inside switch):	301 MBps
Laptop (via wireless):	283 MBps

Note: When I first ran these tests, a few years ago, the results were much lower. When I upgraded my Internet connection, my router was not fast enough. It topped out at 100 MB. So I replaced that and discovered that the wireless access points were another chokepoint. So I replaced them.

. . . and that's exactly the kind of thing you'll find with your clients.

Here's what you record on the form:

1. What's the advertised speed of the network from the ISP?

2. What is the speed just inside the router? Literally plug your laptop into the ISP router and measure the speed. If they have a brand new router, I hope it's fast enough. If it's even a 100MB connection on the inside, it will not step up to the next level when the ISP sells you a faster Internet connection. And you certainly won't be using that router when you switch to fiber.

3. Test the speed inside the firewall. Again, I hope it's a new-ish firewall (Less than three years old). A very old firewall very commonly has a 10MB port on the outside because Internet connections used to be much slower. An old firewall will have only a 100MB port on the outside. That's fine until your Internet connection is 120 or 150 or even gigabit.

Back in the days when a T1 connection gave you 1.5 MB, those slow outside ports were fine. That is now the slowest connection on earth. Well, almost.

If the outside port is 100MB, it doesn't matter if you're paying for a 200MB, you've got a 100MB Internet connection.

And that's exactly what you need to tell your clients.

It's also the case that firewalls that are more than just a couple of years old have old chipsets that can't open packets fast enough to actually provide the speed that's labeled on the network card. So, you have to make sure that the router and the firewall have the right ports and that they're actually performing to what is specified.

It might be that the firewall needs extra memory or that you need an upgrade of some kind.

4. Speed test each port on the switch. If you feel sure that all ports are working fine, you can test just one. But make sure you test the inside of the switch just as you did the inside of the router and firewall.

And if you have teamed network cards on a server, run a speed test on that teamed-NIC to make sure you know what that speed is.

Don't just assume that it's doing what you ask it to do.

5. Test from the wireless access point. You're virtually guaranteed to see a drop-off here. And as more and more networks rely on wireless technology, this final chokepoint will need to be updated on a regular basis.

Repeat this process for the public or insecure wireless network, if the client has one. In many cases, this will be a different device from the secure in-house wireless access. But even if it's the same device, you may have different QOS (quality of service) settings on the two networks.

6. Test inside and outside of QOS devices. For example, if you have a QOS device for voice over IP, it might max out at 100MBps.

The bottom line is to get accurate measurements at every segment of the network(s). You need to be able to have discussions based on verifiable facts.

Heads up: Prepare to enter into an era of arguing with clients about wireless upgrades. As network speeds increase more and more every year, this equipment will become outdated faster than ever. Historically, bandwidth has crept up in speed over time. Those days are gone (no more creeping).

The Client Discussion

Once you have this information, prepare a one-page diagram for each client. You want to be able to visually demonstrate the drop in speed as you go from what they're *buying* to what they're *experiencing*. And then inside the router, inside the firewall, inside the switch, and inside the wireless network.

As I mentioned, I did these speed test for myself several times in 2016, 2017, and 2018 as my bandwidth grew faster and faster. As a result, I have replaced the Internet router and all wireless access points except one. (I maintain a separate network of "Internet of Things" devices, and I don't care if it's slow.)

Please, please, please go through this exercise with every client. I guarantee it will result in sales. It is also an excellent, low-pressure way to begin discussing cloud services and the client's future network needs. Even if you don't sell something today, you will have started the conversation that results in sales tomorrow.

A few quick questions.

Q: What speed test should I use?

A: I don't care what speed test you use. But I encourage you to pick a standard and have all technicians use that.

Q: Should we wait until everyone's off the network?

A: I don't think so. Realistically, measuring bandwidth usage at ten in the morning is probably more accurate than ten at night. If you want to, you could test both.

Remember: We don't really care if the measurement is off by 5 MBps. We care if it drops from 250 MBps to 97 MBps. We're looking for problems with equipment, not human habits.

Q: What's the minimum? What do you recommend as a starting place for Cloud Services?

A: Well . . . That depends.

In a small office with, say, ten users, I would recommend an absolute minimum of 20 MBps bandwidth for the core Cloud Five-Pack™ Offering described in this book.

Yes, that's going to be a little slow and a little painful. But it works. And we've used that configuration on hundreds of users over the last ten years. Having said that, 100MB is a far more common configuration today, and should give excellent performance for almost any office of any size.

Here's my personal "worst case scenario" experience. I travel a lot. I do almost everything in the cloud. Obviously, my email is just better in the cloud. Sometimes it's super-fast and sometimes it's painfully slow. But it's always there and always works. I want my email in the cloud. That's the safest, most reliable place for it to be.

But this is exactly the conversation you need to have with clients. If 10 MBps is all you can get, and it's too slow to open files on a mapped drive in the cloud, then you need to sell them some on site storage and back it up to the cloud. But if they have gigabit fiber, then cloud-based storage is the only thing I'd consider.

I've actually worked in a lot of hotels with horrible Internet. Sometimes it's 4, 5, 6 MB and it is painful. Same with a lot of airplane Internet access. But you can get the job done.

Remember: If you feel like you are frustrated with this Internet connection, your client will be frustrated, and all of their employees will be frustrated. Of course, that level of frustration is going to vary by what they're doing and what they're using it for.

I'm not a fan of "synch" options, but they are excellent for many people. I prefer working direct from the cloud drive. But many services (Dropbox, Apple, eFolder, and others) work great by synchronizing your local folder to the cloud. I would argue that this is best for people who do not need to share lots of individual files with lots of different people.

As always: Your mileage may vary.

Some clients have lots of huge files (e.g., medical images, CAD files, large photos) and you'll need to provide on site storage for them. Most offices will work primarily with Word, Excel, and PowerPoint files. These are much smaller and work great with a drive mapped directly to cloud storage.

As you get in the habit of right-sizing cloud offerings, you will feel much more comfortable with the conversation we're about to have around creating *your* cloud bundle. After all, you know your clients, the normal bandwidth available in your city, and the relevant pricing.

Cloud discussions are not really different from any other business discussion. They involve past experience, budgets, future commitments, work habits, productivity, and new possibilities.

The really good news is that this discussion of bandwidth can open your clients to some great opportunities going forward.

A Few Key Take-Aways:

1. It's easy – and a recommended best practice – to map client bandwidth throughout their network.

2. Network bandwidth audits are a great place to start discussing cloud options and opportunities with clients.

3. Get ready for a period of ever-increasing bandwidth speeds.

Additional Resources to Explore

- Speedtest.net

Notes:

_____

_____

_____

_____

_____

_____

_____

_____

III. Create a Cloud Service Offering

8. Sneak Peek: The Cloud Service Five-Pack

This section has five chapters, all about building and fine-tuning your offering. One of the defining factors that differentiates cloud service providers from managed service providers is The Bundle or The Offer.

Managed services is ultimately about taking ownership of the maintenance of a client's network. To me, managed service consists of the "maintenance of the operating systems and software" (see *Managed Services in a Month*).

Being a cloud service provider means much more than merely adding cloud services to managed services. Personally, I think it is irresponsible to sell un-bundled cloud services. By un-bundled I mean one-off, unrelated, uncoordinated services sold separate from everything else.

Three huge factors are at play here. First, the integrity of a system of technologies lies in the ability of those technologies to work together seamlessly. You can't get that with random elements that you try to force together as a package. Services should be chosen carefully, with intention.

Second, security must be built in to all service offerings at all levels. Security is not a service you bolt on afterward. It needs to be part of the mix from the beginning. Again, that's not likely to happen with products you just threw in the mix.

Third, and we'll come back to this at the end of the book, keeping all the services coordinated and documented is more important than it's ever been. If you lose the password to a physical server, there's still a 99% chance that you'll recover all the data. If data gets lost on the Internet because it's in the wrong person's name, or attached to an email you can't access, that data could be gone forever.

Part of the process of building your bundles is also the process of building a system to track everything, configure everything correctly, document it, and "secure" it from the possibility of simply losing it altogether.

With that intro . . .

Let's Get Building

Okay, let's start building your cloud offering. I will refer to it sometimes as your cloud pack, your Cloud Five-Pack™, or your cloud bundle. As I just mentioned, the bundling concept separates you from just plain old managed service provider who also sells Office 365.

To start off, we're going to walk through how we built the Cloud Five-Pack™ and how it evolved over time. Please note that there are lots of related documents in the download files (see Preface). Some are in PDF format because they are just representations of the evolving bundle. Final versions of everything are in Word documents or other editable formats so you can update them and make them your own.

When we first started pushing cloud services—about 2008—I was running two companies out of the same building, sharing a lot of administrative assistants between the two of them, and just decided, "You know, we should figure out how we can do cloud services and what we want to do." It started out as something for my smallest clients.

On the managed services front, we had moved from a five-user minimum to a 10-user minimum. So, when we looked at our smallest clients, they all had at least ten seats. I think our largest was about 130 seats.

As we started developing the cloud offering, we realized that we could go back down into smaller clients again. This was something we could sell something to people who have only eight, seven, six, five, four users. And, as it turned out, we had more than one client with one or two users who still found value in the five-pack.

I have long had a revenue goal in the neighborhood of a minimum of one thousand dollars per month per client. If they can't find a way to give me a thousand dollars a month, then they need to find somebody else to give them tech support.

At the time, we were charging $350 per month to manage a server and $65 per workstation. So, a client with ten users and a server would pay one thousand dollars. Plus, of course, any add/move/change or project labor.

When we started looking at cloud services, we wondered how we would maintain that goal.

At first, I thought we would design an offering for our smallest clients, perhaps topping out at about twenty users. Note: This incorrect and artificial limit was created because I was using an old mindset about cloud services and comparative value.

Here was my original thinking: If you sell a hosted Exchange mailbox for about $15/month, then at twenty users, the cost is approaching the cost of a hosted Exchange server. So, we thought we'd offer hosted mailboxes to smaller clients and hosted mail servers to larger clients.

But now my thinking is more mature.

I don't want to maintain servers. That's true whether they are in-house servers or hosted servers. I don't want to be responsible for the patches, fixes, updates, service packs, zero-day attacks, antivirus, software updates, hardware updates, etc. All of that takes time, increases downtime, and costs me resources (money and time).

We have sold hosted Exchange mailboxes into businesses with as many as 130 users. I would have no problem going beyond that.

Here's another important factor: With cloud services – especially serverless technology – the price you pay is unrelated to the price you charge.

[Stop: Go back and highlight that last sentence. Really. Put the book down, go find a yellow highlighter, and highlight that sentence.]

The price you charge is unrelated to the price you pay.

This is true for several reasons, and we'll go into this in detail. But for now, look at your business from the client's perspective. What do you do? What do you sell? What service do you provide?

If you say, "I provide servers, and I patch them and fix them and update them," you are not in synch with your clients. Clients don't care about servers or software, or patches and fixes. They care about services. In other words, they want their email to work all the time. They want it to be fast and secure.

The same is true with storage. It should just work. It should be as close to 100% reliable as possible.

So, in terms of *service* and *reliability*, you have to admit that a hosted service is closer to 100% uptime than a physical or virtual server that you maintain. Strictly from the perspective of service, a serverless solution is the way to go. That's your client's view of the world.

The more you accept this reality, the more you realize that you *should* be selling services. And since what you pay and what you charge are not related to each other, you can still charge the same amount you've always charged. You'll just make more money when you resell hosted services that require zero maintenance on your part.

Today I am totally okay to go with the hosted model because it's completely expandable. If you think about it, if you added 100 users (endpoints) to a hosted mailbox system, Microsoft (or Sherweb or Intermedia or Rackspace) would not notice the difference. They have millions of mailboxes. You adding a hundred more will not put a dent in their performance.

Note on Microsoft vs. Google Suite and Others

I fully acknowledge the Microsoft-centric nature of this discussion of Exchange email and office options. Many people make a living setting up clients on Google/G-Suite options.

If you are working with established companies with a long history of using Microsoft Office, you will have no problem convincing them to continue doing so. In fact, you might have a problem convincing them to switch other options.

If you're setting up new offices, especially those made up of individuals who use Google products in the personal lives, then non-Microsoft options may be a better option.

Wherever my discussion seems too one-brand specific, feel free to replace with your favorite brand. In Chapter Twenty-Three we'll discuss creating your catalog of services.

Focus on the Core Technology

Way back in 2006, I wrote a blog post looking at the most fundamental technology that businesses need. Here's the list I came up with:

- Email
- Calendars and collaboration
- Devices (phones, tablets, laptops, etc.)
- Telephones
- Storage / Backup
- "Office" documents

- Printing
- Web site
- Remote monitoring
- Patch management
- Antivirus
- Spam filtering
- Internet connection
  - Firewall
  - Switch
  - Wires in the wall

I don't mention security separately since it needs to be baked in from the start.

Next, I propose the following: Can we create a bundle that provides *All the Technology You Need* in one nice bundle?

And that was the beginning of our cloud offering. We started bundling a lot of this, with the goal to someday bundle all of it. We started by focusing on our smallest client.

But remember that we had a ten-user minimum. So, our bundle actually allowed us to go back into the one-to-nine user clients.

In 2008 when we started implementing this, we identified fifteen clients in the range of ten to thirty users that we wanted to put on our cloud offering right away. Once we starting deploying this bundle, we put all fifteen of those clients on the cloud bundle in one month. We literally moved to being a Cloud Service Provider in 30 Days.

The one thing that clients don't really need is a server. There are certainly good reasons to have a server, especially if you need "classic" Active Directory.* But clients don't need a server to store files in most cases. Cloud storage is a better option. And they don't need a server for email. Cloud-based email is a better option.

Personally, I like a small server (what I call "Server Lite") on site for security, Active Directory, and some kind of local backup from the cloud. But I acknowledge that a server on site is not an absolute requirement.

Clients also don't need to have paper licenses. Clients have always thought, "Oh, I don't want to buy Microsoft Office again. This Office XP is working really great for me." They're reluctant to make upgrades. But, if you can put Office into your cloud bundle, you can easily move them off of volume licensing and make them very "sticky" at the same time.

Clients don't need to buy hard drives, switches, power supplies, and all the hardware components. Those are things that you sold them in order to make the server work. If you ask your clients, "Do you need a hard drive?" they would never say yes.

And to be honest, clients don't need a big phone system bolted to the wall. You can sell them a hosted voice over IP service and it works just as well as what they've got.

Remember when I said we needed to practice zero-based thinking? That's what it looks like. We stopped thinking of ourselves as sellers of hardware, software, and licenses. We started thinking of ourselves as resellers of hosted storage, hosted email, and other hosted services.

* *Classic AD Note:* Microsoft is deploying a new kind of AD, based on Azure and intimately tied to their distributed security initiative. They call it Active Directory Domain Services. See https://docs.microsoft.com/en-us/windows-server/identity/whats-new-active-directory-domain-services. I use the term classic to differentiate the AD model we used from 2000-2018.

Building the First Bundle

In my office, we had a lot of big whiteboards everywhere. In the main conference area, we had one about ten feet wide. We gathered everyone around the conference table, including all of the administrative assistants, technicians, web developers, everybody.

I drew a big box on the board and said, "Okay, what goes in the box? And how much do we charge for it?" At first, we thought the bundle would probably be in the neighborhood of $500 per month. After all, we wanted to include antivirus, spam filtering, storage, and everything on the list above.

We listed out each service to be included. Then we listed the price for one license, three licenses, five licenses, and so forth.

At some point we decided that, at least for now, we wanted the option to have some kind of server on site. Even today, I believe that small businesses will be in a hybrid environment – with some kind of server on site – for at least the next five years.

We'll be moving more and more technology to the cloud, but there will be some things on site for a long time. The good news is: 1) Moving services up to the cloud is easier than moving to new hardware; and 2) Every time you move services up to the cloud, it makes your life easier.

Side Bar: Hybrid Cloud Servers

Just as with "cloud services," there are several definitions of what constitutes hybrid cloud or hybrid services. Let's keep this very simple.

A hybrid model is one that includes both components in the cloud and components on site. With this definition, pretty much all clients are in hybrid environments. They might be 10% cloud and 90% on site or 90% cloud and 10% on site. Or, of course, anywhere in the middle.

There are some products that specifically bill themselves as hybrid solutions. One of them, which I've worked with, was developed by Zynstra. The Zynstra hybrid cloud server is now built into a system sold as HPE's EC200a server.

It runs virtual machines inside the server if you need them, and it manages your licenses for services such as Office 365 and other cloud services.

Certainly, the system we describe with a "Server Lite" on site and pretty much everything else in the cloud is a hybrid model. Similarly, any clients who require a stand-alone physical server for their LOB (line of business application) will be in a hybrid model for some time.

You should be prepared for this hybrid model to last another five or so years. But once the end is in sight, the switch to 100% cloud everything will happen very quickly.

On the next page is a flyer from our first marketing campaign for cloud services. And on the next page is the actual price list for our first **Cloud Five-Pack™**.

As you can see, we offered

- 250 GB of storage
- Five Microsoft Exchange mailbox licenses
- A website
- Remote monitoring and patch management
- Virus scanning
- Spam filtering
- Two hours of in-house training
- and, if they buy the managed service component, then we're going to cover maintenance of the operating system and software

We do include what we call our technology roadmap, which is a meeting with clients to talk about where they are, where they're going, and what they need next. We throw that in and it's basically a consulting for the future that we don't charge them for.

Our price for the bundle was $249 for the Cloud Five-Pack™ and $249 for the managed service component. I think that's the killer combination! Please note, from 2008-2018, we never had a client buy the Cloud Five-Pack™ without buying the managed services component. In other words, nobody ever just buys the Cloud Five-Pack™ with no maintenance.

The reason for this is pretty straight forward: At that price, if they have anything that goes wrong in an entire month, they're going to buy at least two hours of labor, which means they've spent more than if they had bought the managed service component.

Cloud Services "5 Packs"	5 Pack Business in a Box	5 Pack With Managed Service
Managed Storage Space Up To . . .	250 GB	250 GB
Microsoft Exchange Mailboxes	Up to 5	Up to 5
Hosted Web Site – Windows or Unix	Included	Included
User PC Remote Monitoring	Up to 5	Up to 5
Patch Management (apply all critical patches)	Included	Included
User PC Virus Scanning	Up to 5	Up to 5
User Email Spam Filtering	Up to 5	Up to 5
Desktop Support (Maintenance)	$150 / Hr	Included
Remote Project Labor	$150 / Hr	$150 / Hr
Onsite Project Labor	$150 / Hr	$150 / Hr
After Hours Support	$300 / Hr	$300 / Hr
Short Notice Emergency Service (onsite or remote, any time of day)	$300 / Hr	$300 / Hr
Technology Roadmap Process Business Plan and Process Management for Technology	$995	Included
Two Hours Free In-House Training Per Quarter May not be rolled over		Included
Access to Our Emergency Help Line		Included
Monthly Investment Up to Five Users . . .	$249 / Mo	$498 / Mo

I always get asked, "Exactly what does the cloud bundle include, if it doesn't include managed services?" Basically, we're signing them up for all of these services, but if they didn't buy the managed service component then they get no labor. They get no support. If they do sign up for the managed services component, it's exactly what we talked about before – they get maintenance of the operating system and software.

Note (once again) on managed service. For us, managed service covers the maintenance of the operating system and software. That means, it does not include hardware support. It does not include after-hours labor. And it does not cover add/move/change labor.

A Few Key Take-Aways:

1. With cloud services – especially serverless technology – the price you pay is unrelated to the price you charge.

2. You should start working on your cloud bundle!

3. We are very likely to be in a "hybrid" cloud environment for the next five years.

Additional Resources to Explore

*   *Managed Services in a Month* by Karl W. Palachuk

*   **Zynstra** – www.zynstra.com/proliant-easy-connect

9. Server Lite

I have mentioned the "Server Lite" and the hybrid cloud model. Let's look at the Server Lite in more detail.

Way back in 2006, when I wrote about the technology we needed going forward, I was careful to not be looking for a replacement for Small Business Server (SBS). In my opinion, this industry spent far more time and energy bemoaning the demise of SBS than was helpful.

Aside from the Office suite, SBS is the greatest product Microsoft ever produced for the small business market. But by 2006 it was painfully obvious that we were asking a single, under-powered machine to do too much. It was also obvious that cloud services were coming on strong.

SBS 2008 forestalled a lot of problems by allowing us to install a lot more RAM. But you still had a lot going on for one machine. The two-machine premium option also helped. By 2011, it was clear that the end was near for SBS. And Microsoft announced the end of SBS in 2012.

In the meantime, cloud-based (hosted) options were growing quickly. And that changed what we "require" of on site servers. If SQL is hosted, and Exchange is hosted, and storage is hosted, then what do you really need an on site server to do?

To me, it comes down to Active Directory (domain-level security) and a backup from the cloud-based storage.

That's why I started calling the product "Server Lite." Clients and technicians knew what SBS was. We needed to develop a solution that was not operating system specific. So I looked at what this machine needs to do and designed it to do nothing else.

When it came time to start building "Server Lite" machines, I fell in love with the then-new HP Micro Server. This is a little cube-shaped machine built on Proliant technology. I like it with about 16GB RAM and four hard drives.

It has built-in RAID, so you can mirror the C: drive and mirror the D: drive. That makes replacing storage drives very easy.

These machines come pre-configured with various packages of RAM and hard drive options. Just recently, HP stopped shipping Micro Servers with Smart Start configurations for the lighter Windows Servers, so I've moved to other low-end servers. Ah well, everything must come to an end.

Basically, a Server Lite machine should be under one thousand dollars for hardware. Because it does not need redundant memory, redundant power, and fibre connections, you should be able to buy a decent low-enter server around $700.

My favorite operating system has been the OEM Microsoft Essentials, which sells at wholesale for about $325. That makes the whole server plus operating system right in the $1,000-$1,100 range.

I offer this to clients as an appliance. I started out charging $100/month. Now it's normally $150/month. I own this machine and provide it to the client as a service that helps everything in the Cloud Five-Pack™ function well. My pricing goal is to have this machine paid for in seven or eight months.

I love the Server 2016 Essential product. It can only run on "lite" servers. You cannot install Exchange or SQL on it. It comes with 25 user licenses, so there are no CALs (client access licenses) to buy.

The licensing cannot be expanded beyond the 25. Now, having said that, if you need to go past 25, you can install Server 2016 Standard and enable the Essentials role. The Essential Role includes the ability to "connect" and backup home versions of Windows. (Note: Home versions of Windows cannot join a domain, but they can connect to it.) It also gives the client remote access for desktops, including home editions.

But – and it's a big but - once you move to Server Standard plus the Essentials role, you need to buy client access licenses for everything.

With plain old Server Essentials, up to 25 users are allowed. It is a great operating system, and easy to administer. It will automatically set up client machines to back up to the server, if that's what you want to do.

Note: I mentioned above that Server Essentials (2016) has been my favorite option. But with Server 2019, the Essentials server no longer includes the ability to backup desktops or connect remotely to non-pro Windows machines. That doesn't really affect most clients any more. But it's worth noting when you choose an operating system for your Server Lite.

Option One
- Data lives in the Cloud
- Backup down to Server Lite

Option Two
- Data lives on Server Lite
- Backup up to the Cloud

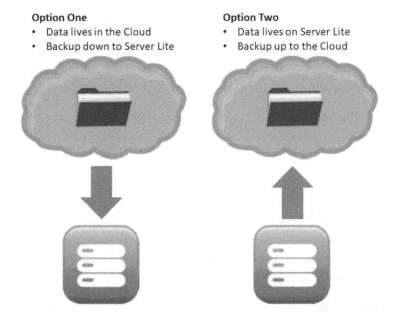

Two Primary Options

There are two options for using Server Lite with regard to data storage and backup. My strong preference is to use the cloud for primary storage. That simply means that all the client's "live" data is in the cloud storage. This takes the place of the old system in which the files sit on a server hard drive.

This is what I have done with all of my companies since 2007. Our primary storage is in the cloud. Every night, we bring a complete copy back down to the Server Lite. On the Server Lite, the drives are mirrored.

The other option is to continue to use the server hard drive for primary storage. This continues to have the disadvantage that users must access the server in order to access their data. Obviously, that's not the case with a cloud drive.

When the server is the primary data store, you then back it up to cloud storage every night.

A few notes. First, you sell the exact same cloud bundle for both of these options. You simply use the cloud storage differently.

Second, it should be obvious why we do not need a big, powerful, beefy server. When all that machine has to do is authenticate logons and backup files from the cloud, it doesn't need much power.

Third, the Server Lite is essentially disposable. You could simply use a NAS (network attached storage) device if you didn't need the Active Directory.

When all your live data is in the cloud, then the local server/storage device becomes a lot less critical. If this server goes down, you can simply backup to another device. In the meantime, no critical functions have stopped. Everyone can get to Exchange, everyone can edit files, everyone can just keep working. Even logons will continue with stored credentials.

If clients have massive local storage needs, or a very slow Internet connection, then you will have to continue using the local server for primary storage. If that's all it does, then you can still get away from expensive hardware (except the hard drives).

Just remember that, as you ask that machine to do more and more, it becomes less "Lite" and requires more maintenance.

One goal of the Server Lite is that you don't have to do a big hour-long monthly maintenance. Instead, you maintain it completely via your RMM tool. Of course you still need to verify that the backup is working. But actual machine maintenance becomes almost nil.

When you let that machine grow to include a database or other critical function, then it needs to go on regular server maintenance because it's no longer lite.

Remember: If your Cloud Five-Pack™ is the bundle you can sell to every single client, and then you add-on whatever else they need, the Server Lite is simply an add-on. And a normal, beefy server that runs a big database is also just an add-on. You need to sell whatever configuration works best for the client.

In my experience, almost all small businesses can use cloud-based primary storage and a Server Lite on site for backup.

Note on Backups: My norm is to replace the data drives once a year. I ask clients to store the old drives securely with their end-of-year financial paperwork.

Reuse That Old Server?

Some clients are ready for cloud services, but they still have a decent, usable server. For example, if you have a Proliant server that's three years old, and it used to be a big SBS Server, that might be a great "Lite" server.

First, you need to extend the warranty just in case. There's no point in running a machine without a warranty. Then you can simply disable Exchange, disable SQL, etc. When you get to the point where the server is doing nothing except authenticating logons and backing up from the cloud, it should be more than enough to get the job done.

Personally, I would not do this on a machine that's five or more years old. At some point, you're just asking for trouble. You'll never be passionate about the Cloud Five-Pack™ if you build it on equipment that's bound to give you trouble.

A Few Key Take-Aways:

1. There are two primary storage methods. I highly recommend keeping primary storage in the cloud and backing up by bringing a copy down every night.

2. Server Lite can be any lightweight server because it does very little work.

3. If you have a good server with some life left in it, that can serve as your Server Lite until it needs to be replaced.

Additional Resources to Explore

- Again, I don't really have a resource to point to here. But I encourage you to check out my Community at www.smallbizthoughts.org. Thanks.

10. Plan Changes and Updates

Of course our plan evolved over time. The plan we first introduced was just enough to get started. You may choose to do the same thing, or you may choose to have a much more inclusive offering.

In this chapter, we're going to cover how we price the Five-Pack, how we make money, what the back end looks like, and how we make changes to the bundle. Let's start by looking at the COGS – the Cost of Goods Sold – for the cloud bundle.

For our original cloud bundle, here were the COGS:

Cost of Good Sold - Cloud Five-Pack™ v. 1 (circa 2008)

Storage – Up to 250 GB	$30.00
Exchange Mailbox x5	37.50
Basic Web site hosting	1.00
Remote Monitoring x5	7.50
Antivirus x5	5.00
Total COGS	$81.00

There are lots of explanatory notes for this simple table. Let's look at each service in turn.

Disclaimer: When I mention brands for any services in this book, please note that I am NOT being paid to mention anyone. I'm just reflecting my experience and knowledge. At some point I have done business with or received money from almost every service or product mentioned in this book. But I have worked to provide a straight-forward and honest discussion of all products and services. There are no "paid placements" here.

For storage, we started out using Jungle Disk with Amazon storage. We moved to Rackspace for two reasons. First, they both charge the same thing for data storage (data at rest), but Amazon also charges for data in transit (moving to and from storage). Second, Rackspace offered other services, including hosted Exchange mailboxes. So it was easy to buy additional services from them.

Jungle Disk is a service that connects cloud storage with a little applet that runs on your computer and maps it to a drive letter. It also provides file versioning and backup. You can use it to synchronize folders and provide backups. We use it primarily as a drive mapping service.

Note that Jungle Disk eliminated their reseller program at some point, so we developed procedures to implement it without the reseller program. They have recently (2018) re-started their reseller program. Because they have some significant minimum charges to get started, you might want to try the service without going through the reseller program.

Note also that the 250 gigs of storage is literally never used up by one client. We put the price estimate of $30 as the worst-case scenario in case someone does manage to use all of it. Remember, when they go over five users, they buy another five-pack and get another 250 GB of storage.

Back when we started, the average small business had about 6-10 GB of company data per employee. So that amounts to 60-100 GB for a ten-person shop. Unless a client works with CAD design or some other specialty program, they are not likely to approach the 250 GB limit for five people.

For **Hosted Exchange mailboxes**, our cost was about $7.50 each. So five of them is $37.50. You'll see how this pricing evolved over time as Microsoft's O365 pricing changed.

The **basic website** is listed for one dollar. That's really just a holding place. When we dig into options, you'll see that it costs me less than that. I have been using DreamHost for web hosting for more than ten years. Of course there are other hosting providers who are also competitive.

What we offer there is what I call a five-page brain-dead web site. If the client wants us to copy over a small HTML site, we do that. If they want a WordPress site, we install WordPress and point the first user to them. We do not include any programming or labor of any kind in this.

If they want a fancier site, they need to hire a web developer. And, as you know, most web developers prefer to host the site as well for a lot more money. In the end, most of our clients never used the web site we included.

Profit is . . . Excellent!

Remember, we are selling a five-pack of licenses here. But we only buy as much as we deploy. So we don't buy all that storage. We only buy what the client uses. The same is true with RMM licenses, Exchange licenses, etc. The $81 estimate is our worst case (least profitable) scenario.

So, in 2008, it would cost us *at most* $81 to provide $249 worth of services. And then we added the managed service component for an additional $249. Our total profit, in the worst-case scenario, was $417 out of $498 – **roughly 83%**.

We set the original price based on what it would cost us to provide all services without good, automated tools. In other words, if we didn't have automated patch management and we had to go out there and run Microsoft updates and verify that everything worked every month, we would still be profitable.

As soon as you have to spend labor, of course, your profit goes down. But look at the list. Other than approving patches and managing the RMM software, there's really nothing here that requires labor. Stuff just works.

My team put fifteen clients on this program in thirty days, and our profit literally jumped up.

Now let's look at how we improved it.

Making Changes to the Cloud Five-Pack™

A few years later, our offering had changed a bit. Now we offered:

Storage – up to 250 GB

Exchange Mailbox – up to five users

Spam Filtering – up to five mailboxes

Basic Web site hosting

Remote Monitoring – up to five machines

Patch Management – up to five machines

Microsoft Office Pro – up to five users

Technology Roadmap process

Two hours of training per quarter

The price remained $249 for the Five-Pack plus $249 for the managed services.

The big change here is that we are including Office 365, sold through Rackspace or Intermedia at the time. (Also available from Sherweb, AppRiver, and many other vendors.)

Personally, I don't like the Microsoft O365 direct reselling interface and dashboard. I find it to be more labor-intensive administration than I want to do. That means I pay more for my license, and I'm calculating that I'll save the difference because I spend less time dealing with the dashboard.

Until about 2014, we could not make money selling Office 365, so we didn't sell it. Eventually, being able to sell though a reseller such as Intermedia or Sherweb allowed us to buy O365 and lots of other services from one convenient portal.

This reseller model also means that WE run the credit card. We own the client. The client has no idea what we pay for O365. We simply include it in the bundle and everyone's happy.

The move to include Office had two significant impacts. First, it reduced our gross profit somewhat. Instead of paying about $7.50 per mailbox, we were now paying about $12.50 for the suite (mailbox plus office products).

But the second impact was extremely positive for us. We simply told clients that we were now able to include Office licenses on all their machines . . . and upgraded everyone to the latest version. The benefits here are tremendous.

We no longer have offices with a little Office XP, a few Office 2003 machines, a few Office 2012 . . . etc. Now everyone has 2016. Or whatever the latest version is.

That, in turn, means that we eliminate thousands of end-points with security holes for viruses to get in. Having a completely-uniform environment across one office is awesome. Having a completely uniform environment across 98% of your client base is unbelievable.

Side Bar on Viruses

I have a phrase I use when clients ask me about the latest virus scare or ransomware: "You're my client. You're not eligible for that virus."

The only place I've ever seen a crypto-virus is in a PowerPoint presentation at a conference. I believe this is due to a small set of factors. 1) No one in my client base has administrative privileges. So even if they "elevate" their privileges, they can only go so far. 2) All machines and all software is patched on a regular basis. So there are no holes to take advantage of. 3) No machines are running old operating systems. Again, no holes to take advantage of. 4) Client training!!! See what I do in this video: http://bit.ly/sbtsecure.

I believe, because I've done it, that you can run a virus-free environment for a decade if you commit yourself to it. When you let your clients tell you how to do your job, you open the door to security holes. Yes, it's due in part to client training, but that's time well spent.

Okay. I'm stepping off my soapbox.

My general strategy with updates is to cycle through a series of changes. First, there's the basic offering. Then you add something to the offering, making it more valuable. The next year, you increase the price. Then, the year after that, you increase your hourly rate. The year after that, you add something to the bundle.

Rinse. Repeat. Got it?

So here's what we did. We included Office Pro (equivalent). Note that that does not include MS Access. So if a client needed Access, we would charge extra for that. I hope you see where this is going. The next feature update will include Access. In the meantime, we increased our hourly rate and increased the price of the Cloud Five-Pack™.

We moved the price to $299 for the five-pack and $299 for managed services. I see no reason to make these different prices. It's really easy to just say "X" for one offering and "X" for the managed services.

Next, in 2017, our offering looked like this:

> Storage – up to 250 GB
>
> Exchange Mailbox – up to five users
>
> Spam Filtering – up to five mailboxes
>
> Basic Web site hosting
>
> Remote Monitoring – up to five machines
>
> Patch Management – up to five machines
>
> Microsoft Office Pro – up to five users
>
> MS Access if needed – up to five users
>
> Email archiving if needed – up to five users
>
> Email Encryption if needed – up to five users
>
> Technology Roadmap process
>
> Two hours of training per quarter

The price stayed at $299 for the Five-Pack plus $299 for the managed services.

What we did here is to add in MS Access if someone needed (so now the offering was equivalent to an Office Pro Plus open license). We also added a few niceties: Email archiving and email encryption.

Please note: All of these additions are on an as-needed basis. If an office has 27 employees, but only six use Access, then we only pay for six Access licenses. Similarly, most people don't need email encryption or archiving.

As you can see, the number of un-used licenses goes up as you offer more services. The difference between potential licenses in use and actual licenses in use is an important part of your profit here.

One reason we were able to add all these goodies is the changing nature of what Microsoft and the resellers offer. In this case, Intermedia started selling a bundle for $12.50 that includes Outlook, public folders, ActiveSync, and spam filtering. We added encrypted email, archiving, and then a company-wide disclaimer (email signature for the entire domain).

Remember: One of the important rules for long term success with managed services is to flatten the bill as much as possible. Clients love it when they get one invoice and it doesn't have lots of little independent charges.

Now, here's our current cost of goods sold:

Cost of Goods Sold - Cloud Five-Pack™ v. 1 (circa 2017)

Storage – Up to 250 GB	$35.00
Exchange/Office Bundle x5	$62.50
Email encryption x5	$37.50
Email Archiving x5	$15.00
Company disclaimer x1	$12.50
Access Database x5	$19.00
Basic Web site hosting	1.00
Remote Monitoring x5	7.50
Antivirus x5	5.00
Total COGS	$195.00

As for profit, remember that the $195 is a worst-case scenario. In fact, it's extremely unlikely that costs would ever be that high. But even at that, we sell this bundle with managed services for $599, and the profit is $404. That's just over 67% profit.

Quite realistically, our profit is over 70% on this bundle. There are several reasons for this.

In the next chapter, I'll dig into all the details that make profit higher. But I wanted this chapter to focus on the core elements of pricing, COGS, and profit.

A Few Key Take-Aways:

1. Your cloud bundle should be very profitable. Focus on the *value* clients receive, not your costs.

2. Revise your bundle, raise your hourly rates, and raise the bundle price on a rotating basis.

3. Only deploy as many licenses as you actually need.

Additional Resources to Explore

- Example client training on security – https://www.youtube. com/watch?v=LSRkV4XylRg

- **Intermedia** – www.intermedia.net

- **Rackspace** – www.rackspace.com

- **Sherweb** – www.sherweb.com

- **Jungle Disk** – www.jungledisk.com

Notes:

11. Transactions, Customers, and Clients

Wherein we shall explore the mantra:

Stop Selling New Stuff the Old Way!

I have presented this pricing model to over a thousand IT professionals all over the world. There are lots of questions about the money side of things. So this chapter is intended to dig into the philosophy and mentality behind the Cloud Five-Pack™ pricing model.

The road to poverty is paved with bad advice. And where do you get this advice? In our industry, the most common answer is your vendors. After that it's online forums where anyone can say anything they want.

Vendors don't intend to give bad advice. But they're working from their own perspective. They want you to keep your prices low so they can sell more product. They stand up at conferences and promise you seven or ten percent margins. As you saw in the last chapter, I want you to figure out how to go from 67% margin to 70% margin.

Forum folks are also well intentioned. But very often, they are repeating someone else's advice. And, you never know if the person giving you this advice is massively successful or just scraping by.

So, take advice with a grain of salt. Even though every word I write is absolutely true for me, you should also put my advice into the context of your business, your clients, and your experience.

Now let's explore some of the philosophy behind the Cloud Five-

Pack™ that has allowed me to sell millions of dollars' worth of cloud services over the last ten years.

Unused Licenses are Gold

It's a mathematical truth that only 20% of your clients have a number of employees exactly divisible by five. And therefore, 80% of your clients will have unused licenses with the Cloud Five-Pack™.

For example, a client with 27 employees will buy six five-packs. And again, the same way we talked about managed service pricing, you buy whatever you need and then you sell one and two at a time. With the Five-pack, you'll have lots of unused licenses that accumulate across your clients. And, again, you buy only the licenses that you need to deliver.

But wait. It gets better!

We basically assume that clients will top out at about five devices per person. So, for example, an attorney might have a desktop computer, a laptop, a smart phone, a tablet, and a home computer that you support.

And in an office with, say, seven attorneys and five assistants, you might have two principle partners that are super-users like that. The other attorneys have three or four devices each.

And the paralegals and office assistants? Most likely, they have one device per person. They don't have company laptops, you don't support their home machines, and they're not allowed to have email on their phone.

In total, you've got two super users, five power users, and five basic users. So, even though you've deployed a total of twelve licenses, five of them are essentially self-maintaining. That is, nothing ever goes wrong with their stuff because they just have one PC each. As long as your RMM works, and everything except Office is in the cloud, these folks don't have anything that breaks.

Now consider that 27-person office above. They also probably have two or three super-users. And they probably have about five to ten power users. Which means they have at least fifteen basic, one-device users.

As the size of the client increases, the percentage of basic users increases. In fact, in my experience, the number of super-users and power users tops out around fifteen to twenty per company. That's true with fifty users, and 100, and 150.

But wait. It gets better.

When you look at the goodies we've added to the bundle, the things that cost us extra money, they follow the same pattern.

It is extremely rare to have an office with fifty employees who all need MS Access. Unless it's the basis for a company-wide line of business application, there will be a limited number of people who need it.

Email archiving is the same way, as is email encryption.

So, as the size of the company grows, the number of unused licenses goes up. In fact, the disparity can become so large that you end up lowering the price of the five-pack after a client buys a certain number.

I haven't done that, but you might.

Note: The largest client we've had on the Cloud Five-Pack™ was 130 users.

When clients get large, you also have the option to set up basic email (not Exchange mailboxes) on the same domain. These are significantly cheaper for users that don't need to access calendars, public folders, etc. Note that this option is not available if you're selling direct from Microsoft. But resellers such as Intermedia and Sherweb offer non-Exchange mailboxes on the same domain as Exchange mailboxes.

Remember:

Stop Selling New Stuff the Old Way!

But My Clients Can Count

I always get the objection that clients won't pay for ten licenses when they're only using eight.

Truth: I get that question from technicians. But I have never had that question from a client or prospect. It's a thing *we* worry about. But if you sell it right, the client never worries about it.

It's very important that you promote this bundle as "Up to five users" for each of the services. That's critical.

This pricing really is the same technique as Netflix: Up to five individual profiles per account. No one ever complains that they only have three family members, so they shouldn't have to pay for five profiles. Why? Because Netflix allows their account to have up to five profiles.

The buyer isn't losing anything by paying $599 for all the technology their entire office needs. In fact, that's a pretty good deal!

Also, if you think you need to prepare for this objection, consider the best argument for bundles in general. It is the bundled package that allows you to provide truly trouble-free services. The bundle allows you to keep the price down. You have hand selected the components so they all work together.

The next objection is often, "Do you really charge someone the full price for a 6th user?" Short answer: Yes.

Again, I've never had a client question this. But in my head, I justify it because I rely on the client's administrator email account for a lot of hard work. Here's what I mean.

Best Practice: Use the Client's Administrator Email Account

I have always run my business in such a manner that the client can get rid of me and the next technician can come up to speed as quickly and easily as possible. One element in this is that we use the client's administrator email to register all hardware, all software, extended warranties, domain names, etc.

This means I have to create an administrator email box on the client's domain. Very often, I will set up "basic" mailboxes that do not require an Exchange license.

But the important thing is that the email address administrator@company.com is used for lots of record keeping and product registration. So it's important to the company – as if it were a "real" user.

On the few occasions when we've resold Office 365 directly, I have created email aliases and registered the users in the format

- workstation01@company.onmicrosoft.com
- workstation02@company.onmicrosoft.com
- workstation03@company.onmicrosoft.com

Each of these is an alias for the administrator email. If I need a password reset, I can simply request it and then check the administrator email to verify.

This is also handy when people move around. Instead of having to remove Bob and add Carol to a machine just to keep licenses straight, I do nothing – because the registration email for the workstation stays the same.

Anyway, I just never have to argue about the licenses with prospects. Only computer consultants.

As I mentioned earlier, I had set a five-user minimum way back around 2000, and eventually I set a ten-user minimum. Now, with the Cloud Five-Pack™, I was selling into that 1-9 market again. I literally had to relearn how to deal with the smallest clients.

I found that I could sell a five-pack to people with as few as one person because, especially early on, $250 a month is so cheap, no one argued with it. Again: "All the technology you need for only $250 a month."

And everyone bought the managed service component because that labor is pretty cheap as well. When a client has almost any issue, it's easy to spend two hours a month in labor. Well, two hours of our labor costs more than the $250 or $300 we charged for the managed service component.

Now you may ask, don't we lose money when we're only charging $300 for all the labor? Of course not. Remember, we have rules. There is no such thing as "All you can eat." We never use that phrase.

In fact, we are vigorous in pushing the definition of managed services as "Maintenance of the operating system and software." That means hardware is not covered.

And as for the list of services we provide, nothing breaks. Really. Office doesn't break. Cloud storage doesn't break. Antivirus doesn't break. And so forth. Nothing breaks. Really. Ever.

Remember, there really is a magic formula to keep a client up and online all the time. It's very simple:

1. All machines need to be "new" – which is to say, three years or less
2. All machines need to be under warranty
3. Clients should be running the latest operating system
4. All software needs to be new – which means the latest version
5. All systems need to be patched, fixed, and updated
6. All software needs to be patched, fixed, and updated
7. All machines need protection from viruses and malware

Replacing one third of all machines each year is outside the scope of my Cloud Five-Pack™ – but I would be totally open to creating a plan that included it.

Other than that, we have accomplished most of this checklist with the Cloud Five-Pack™ bundle. And guess what? If machines are out of warranty, then they're not covered by managed service. So any problems with those machines would be billable.

As for the services, I can remember one outage with Jungle Disk (actually Rackspace storage on Jungle Disk) in the last twelve years. There might have been a blip in the middle of the night, but I count one real outage that affected me or my clients.

Similarly, I have not had problems with Intermedia, Rackspace, AWS, Azure, Sherweb, or other providers. I have had minor issues with hosted web sites, mostly related to me moving my web sites to a new virtual server. But with any of these services, *you* can't actually fix anything. You open a ticket and they fix their stuff.

Another important rule that saves us money: We have a clause in our contract that states that all work on their systems has to be done by us and our employees. It can't be done by the client or anyone else that they hire. And if we have to fix something that somebody else did, it's billable. So even if it would have been covered by managed services, it's billable if we don't do the work.

Like everyone else, we are subject to Microsoft pushing an update that screws up Outlook or some other product. Luckily, we have our RMM agent on all machines, so we can uninstall the offending update very easily across all clients. And, in that regard, we're affected as much or as little as any other managed service provider.

Remember:

Stop Selling New Stuff the Old Way!

Don't Sell Cloud Services Like Break/Fix

In the next few chapters, we'll talk about pricing strategies. But here I want to make sure we're clear on the beauty of the bundle – including managed services.

As you've seen, I wax poetic about the bundled offering. There really is some magic there. And the cloud services plus managed services combination is even better.

Sell this bundle as your core offering. Make it the one thing you can sell to every single client. Then you can add additional services as needed. If someone really needs a local server for their line of business, that's fine. Sell them Cloud Five-Pack™s and add-on a server under managed services.

But do not take apart the bundle!

Use the bundle to help sell the bundle. You can tell prospects that you'll get rid of their separate bills for antivirus, Office 365, email, etc. A good chunk of the cost for the Five-pack will come from money saved on separate services.

And never, ever, ever set people up on cloud services and walk away. That is literally setting them up in a break/fix environment. If you set up a client on Office 365 without the bundle, then they are no longer your client. They don't pay you and you don't see much money. More importantly, they could be gone in a minute.

The same is true when you set people up on cloud storage and all the other services. If you are not collecting the money from the client, they are not your client.

Even worse, you have left the client in exactly the situation all of this is intended to avoid. They now have six or seven invoices from disparate companies, a mish mash of services that may or may not work great together, and no ongoing support to make sure everything keeps working.

You need to believe that the bundle is the right thing to do. You select services that work great together. You configure them all, document them all, and create processes and procedures to make sure it is as seamless as possible for the client.

Then you support them. Your RMM keeps everything patched and updated. You bill everything through your system. The client has a relationship with you. YOU are the cloud service provider for everything they need.

Of course you make money doing that. And that's perfectly fair. You have created a system that brings much higher value than a random collection of cloud services. Your system is worth the price.

Instead of a series of never-ending transactions, you have beautiful bundle and a client who relies on you to keep their business humming along.

Remember:

Stop Selling New Stuff the Old Way!

Quick Note on the Microsoft-Centric Model

You may note that we do not use SharePoint or OneDrive for the hosted storage. This is a personal bias on my part.

These are included in the Office 365 licenses, and we'll set them up if clients ask. But I find SharePoint to be very clunky compared to a nice, simple mapped drive letter. If all you need is storage, I'm not going to steer you toward SharePoint.

Similarly with OneDrive, I find it cumbersome to administer, so we don't deploy it. With clients on a domain, you can use a group policy to disable it so that nobody accidentally ever stores anything there.

One of the great dangers of the 21st century is that people are going to lose control of their own data. Some of it is ransomware. There will be companies who refuse to pay for the ransomware and all their data will be gone, and that is no different than if their hard drive crashed or fell in the ocean. They're done.

The other problem is the opposite, which is to say, their data is everywhere. Employees put some data on OneDrive, some on Dropbox, etc. Now the company doesn't control the data, and doesn't even know where it is.

More about this later in the book. For now, just know that you should have *one* cloud storage option and stick with it.

A Few Key Take-Aways:

1. Unused licenses are gold. They flatten the client's monthly spend and guarantee you consistent revenue.

2. Stop having both sides of the conversation: Don't worry about clients obsessing on unused licenses. They won't.

3. Love your bundle: Stop selling new stuff the old way.

Additional Resources to Explore

- **Amazon Web Services** – aws.amazon.com/partners/channel-reseller

- **Azure (Microsoft)** – www.WindowsAzure.com

- **DropBox** – www.dropbox.com

- **Jungle Disk** – www.jungledisk.com

- **Microsoft OneDrive** – onedrive.live.com

- **Office365** – products.office.com

- **Rackspace** – www.rackspace.com

- **Sherweb** – www.sherweb.com

12. Managed Services and Cloud Services

I have hinted at the fact that I consider Managed Services plus Cloud Services to be the Killer Combo. In fact, some readers have heard me make that exact claim in presentations.

Here's why I'm so passionate about this: If you were to set your sites on providing a perfect network, which never failed, and always provided the client with the greatest support possible, I believe you could achieve that with cloud services plus managed service.

Many of us in this business spend our time bemoaning the fact that servers go down, hard drives fail, and clients get viruses. But it doesn't have to be that way. Really, honestly. In the 2020s there is absolutely no reason for these things to be common at any client office.

I firmly believe that those are complaints of the 2000s – not the 2020s. And that's because too many people are delivering hardware, software, and services exactly the way they did fifteen years ago.

You know the old saying: Keep doing what you've done and you'll keep getting what you got.

There's a new way of delivering the best services possible. And it's not just because it's new, but because it really is the right thing to do.

For example, almost no one today would recommend that we install Windows Server with a dedicated Exchange server into a client office with ten desktops. With quality equipment, that's at least a $5,000 project. And all we've really achieved is email!

With Small Business Server, that was the right solution in 2000, 2005, and even 2010. But today it is no longer the right solution.

It costs too much. It puts too much of a burden on the client's network. It is less accessible when there's an Internet connectivity issue.

In short: There are lots of reasons that the old way of doing things is no longer the right way of doing things. And we as an industry need to stop selling things the old way.

The "perfect" network would have machines that never fail. How do you achieve that? Here's how:

- Replace 1/3 of all machines every year, so everything is always under warranty

- Only sell business class equipment, so it should be trouble free for those three years

- Only run with the latest software. Generally, this is achieved with recurring licenses so you always have the latest version.

- Always install all patches and updates in a timely manner. That's true for hardware, operating systems, and software.

- Always run a virus scanner. But note that 99.999% of all viruses have to take advantage of an unpatched hole in the hardware, OS, or software.

- Monitor everything and respond quickly if something is out of whack

Sound too good to be true? It's not. Not remotely. In fact, there are many, many companies that have provided exactly this combination of services for more than a decade.

Today, the magic combination that makes all this happen is a rigid set of processes and procedures, combined with cloud-based software and services, and regular managed services. Really.

It really is that simple. I've done it. But so have thousands of others. In truth, there's no magic here at all. It's just a matter of putting together the right package and delivering what you promise.

Many years ago, the entire small business consulting community was in an uproar about how poorly Windows Vista performed. I never witnessed this. I never had a single performance issue with Vista. When I mentioned it one time, a Microsoft MVP replied with a smile, "That's because you never install new operating systems on old hardware."

True enough. One of our little rules for success is that we don't mix new operating systems with old hardware or new hardware with old operating systems. Similarly, we never sell used or refurbished equipment.

Most of the time, those things won't be troublesome. But what is most of the time? Let's say it's 80%. That means that twenty percent of the time, you've got a train wreck to deal with. I don't want that – ever. So I don't do those things.

My point is simply this: We can achieve nearly-perfect networks with nearly-perfect performance.

Some of you don't have the faith that your clients will invest in that. Some of you simply don't believe me. Some of you think you'll fail and go bankrupt if you try to push quality systems and maintenance on your clients.

Maybe you're right. But I recommend that you give it a try. Who knows? You might have an incredibly lucrative business model that makes your company a lot of money over the next five to ten years.

Stop selling new stuff the old way.

Stop letting vendors tell you how to run your business!

Microsoft and Amazon are making record profits. Are you getting your share? There's a Cloud Services Gold Rush going on. Where's your share?

Break It Down

Let's take a look at this killer combo.

Lesson One (from the last hundred pages): *Serverless* services provide better performance and give you ongoing revenue with lower maintenance costs. So, sell hosted services not hosted servers.

Lesson Two: Bundle everything! Create a cloud bundle that you can sell as "All the technology a client needs." Get as close to that as possible, and then add-on services and hardware as needed.

> Example Bundle: Exchange hosted mailboxes, storage, spam filtering, antivirus, Office products, web site, remote monitoring, patch management, backup, and managed services.

Lesson Three: Have a great managed service offering. Never "all you can eat," but flatten the bill as much as you can.

Managed services means much more than flat rate services. It means a complete and total focus on preventive maintenance. Patch everything, all the time. Prevent viruses. Make systems "ineligible" for ransomware. Test backups. Do everything you need to do to prevent problems.

And here's why it looks like magic . . . New machines have fewer holes. New operating systems have fewer problems. New software has fewer problems. And you spend a lot less time making new stuff work with new stuff than you would if you had old stuff in the mix.

So, here's what happens. The machines don't break. The operating system doesn't break. The software doesn't break. The cloud services don't break. You use great tools – such as a world class RMM – and automate maintenance.

Nothing breaks. Really.

Where People Go Wrong

What is that ideal operating environment worth to a client? Well, in round numbers, let's say **a lot more than a system that breaks!**

If the old system took ten hours of labor per month and cost the client $1,500/month, then this system is more valuable than the old system. We don't raise the price. In fact, we try to keep it right at what they were paying before. But we make more profit because we don't have to run all over town fixing things.

Too many people break up the bundle. That's a huge mistake. When you start looking at the individual pieces, you lose the value of the whole.

When you look at individual pieces, you start taking on the vendors' view of markup. You look at a mailbox that costs you $7.50 and charge $10 for it. Then you look at storage that costs you $35 and you charge $50.

And one piece at a time you have talked yourself down to barely getting by.

That sounds cheaper for the client, but it's not. Because now you don't have the luxury of making sure that everything's patched and updated. Now you feel you have to charge to test backups, or you don't have time to do it.

Your perfect system starts falling apart as soon as you start questioning the bundle. It really is the case that you can create and maintain a perfect system – if you do it right. As soon as you start cutting corners, then you let in errors and problems and imperfections.

If you have a bundle that works, you earn enough money to do all the maintenance (mostly patching and monitoring). If you charge too little, then you fall back into a break/fix model. More on that in the next chapter.

Too many people sell cloud services like break/fix. In other words, they set up a client system with all the goodies, and then they walk away. No patches, no updates, no testing backups.

First of all, I believe this is simply bad service. Installing systems and walking away is the opposite of providing good service.

Second, you get no money as the system hums along and little holes appear because no one is patching them. In other words, you lose money as the client's system deteriorates.

Third, when there's a problem, it's likely to be a big one. And the client is likely to call whoever comes to mind. If it's you, they might argue that you set up a system with flaws, so they want free labor. If it's not you, then someone else gets the money to fix stuff.

In either case, you have created the perfect break/fix environment: You only make money because your client's system is down or having trouble.

I personally believe that this is actually a matter of morality. Once you know that there's a good, right way to maintain client systems, you have an obligation to offer that. Otherwise, you've created systems in which you only make money when the people who rely on you are losing money.

There's a certain irony here. When you or the client want to take the route that looks cheap, you might make 10% profit. When you do the right thing and create the nearly-perfect network, you make 70% profit and the client has zero downtime.

I know this sounds a bit preachy. But I really believe there's a right way to deliver services. And once you know about it, I believe you should take the route of building systems that provide extreme uptime and are as trouble-free as possible.

Stop selling servers. On site or in the cloud.

Stop selling on site backups.

Stop maintaining servers. Sell hosted services instead.

Stop selling new stuff the old way.

Break/Fix and Hybrid Models

In modern IT consulting businesses, there are generally three types of labor you sell. Depending on your business model, you will define the "type" of business you are based on where you get most of your (labor) money. These three categories are:

1. Hourly Labor is literally labor sold by the hour. You might wrap it up into blocks of time. You might get paid in advance or paid in arrears. But this category is defined as trading dollars for hours.

2. Flat Fee Labor is usually a form of project labor. It might also be used for setup fees. Basically, you quote a specific *per job* price and then stick to it. Profitability is determined by how well you manage the project.

3. Managed Service Labor is any hours worked in support of a managed service contract. How you determine the rate is worthy of a few chapters in a few books. But the overall model is one that assumes you will be using tools and processes to provide a specific value to the client. If your process and tools are good, you make money. If not, you make less money.

You might not consider yourself a pure-play managed service provider, but almost everyone makes money from some recurring, managed labor.

Another type of revenue we get that may be sold as a "service" involves little or no labor at all: Hosted services. For example, a hosted Exchange mailbox or a web site may be provided to the client and billed as a service.

In any given month, you probably expend no labor supporting these services, but you still collect the service fee. Obviously, this is what we're selling in the Cloud Five-Pack™.

So, what's your business model?

Do you call yourself a managed service provider? A break/fix or unmanaged consultant? A cloud service provider? Something else?

The truth is, I don't care what you call yourself. But I would love to have you move to a model with lots of recurring revenue, and to make hourly labor the smallest piece of that pie. The reason is very simple: Hourly labor limits your income. The other services do not.

No matter what you charge per hour, you can only bill so many hours per month. And you can kid yourself and even lie to yourself about how billable you are. Thirty years of experience and thousands of hours working with IT providers all over the world give me a very good idea of what you can expect.

Your billable hours will top out at around 1,000 hours per year for a one-person shop. That's the top. A good technician will bill somewhere in the neighborhood of 1,200-1,600 hours per year.

By "bill" I mean productive labor. So it might be hours worked on a managed service contract or hours billed by the hour. That works out to about 60-80% billable.

This is normal and expected. After all, you have to do sales. You might not charge for drive time. You can't invoice a client for your company meetings. There is *overhead time* to run a business. And as a result, you'll be lucky if your entire tech team as a whole is in the range of 60-70% billable.

The beautiful thing about flat-fee projects is that you can almost guarantee yourself the high end of the billability distribution. (For details on how to do that, see my book with Dana Goulston, *Project Management in Small Business*.)

But the real juicy profit is in managed services, where you break away from the "per hour" calculation altogether. With managed services, you focus on the value of what you're providing. And, as we saw in the last chapter, combining managed services and cloud services is the Killer Combo.

Almost no one gets the majority of their money from flat-fee projects. I encourage you to sell flat-fee projects, but you really need to focus on hourly labor and managed services to determine which business model you're using.

One of my coaching clients worked with lots of dentists. As he described it, dentists pay huge amounts for their dental equipment, and it comes with a lifetime of maintenance. The price for lifetime maintenance is baked into the price of the equipment.

As a result, dentists he works with are reluctant to commit to a large managed service contract for desktop PCs, tablets, etc. So, he sells them a very small service that gives him a small stream of recurring revenue. But he gets to put his RMM agent on everything and sell them hourly labor for anything that goes wrong.

His "managed service" revenue is less than twenty percent of his total revenue per client. My model is almost exactly the opposite. I like to sell a large managed service deal and estimate that another 10-15% will come in as hourly labor.

We both collect about the same total income per workstation per year. So both models work. But his business is "primarily hourly" while mine is "primarily managed service." We are both managed service providers.

And, in fact, we would both say that every single client is a managed service client. But the mix of recurring revenue and hourly labor is opposite.

In some sense, even those of us who are die hard fans of managed services have to admit that we're in a hybrid model. I'm much closer to "all" managed services. Others are closer to an all-hourly model.

Now Add Cloud Services

Assuming you are somewhere within such a hybrid mix, the move to cloud services should increase your revenue significantly – without requiring you to hire more staff.

Think of the transition in steps. First, you do break/fix. This is literally reactive tech support. You wait until something breaks, then you fix it.

Second, you move to providing regular maintenance. You're still paid by the hour, but you focus on patching and updating *before* things break. As a result, the client experiences less downtime. They see the value of preventive maintenance.

Third, you move the client to managed services. Now you've flattened the client's bill and provided even more reliability. Almost nothing ever goes wrong, and you make recurring revenue.

Fourth, you move the client to cloud services. They pay you about the same, but there is almost nothing left to break. You get a "managed service" fee for the desktop environments and you manage all the cloud services.

You can short-cut this by moving straight to cloud services at any point. But if you haven't got clients addicted to preventive maintenance, it might be a harder sell. And if you avoid bundling, you give up all the juicy profit.

The bundle really is the thing!

-- -- --

Enough money talk. Let's start migrating to the cloud!

The next section covers both the approach to migration and lots of details. Combined with the checklists in the resources section, this should give you a great start.

A Few Key Take-Aways:

1. The nearly-perfect network really is possible

2. Bundles are magic

3. Cloud services plus managed services is the Killer Combo

Additional Resources to Explore

- Video: Don't Sell Cloud Services the wrong way - https://www.youtube.com/watch?v=KFkXZhUULHw

- *Project Management in Small Business* by Dana Goulston and Karl W. Palachuk

IV. Migrating to the Cloud

13. One Service at a Time

The beautiful thing about moving to cloud services is that you can migrate each service independent of all the other services.

Back in the days of physical "server migration" projects, many people would take over the client's office, shut the old server down on Friday night, put in the new server, move everything over, and hope that they were done when the sun came up on Monday morning. That was the norm for most of the SMB community worldwide.

My brother Manuel and I developed an entire migration strategy that allows you to move from one set of hardware to another with zero downtime. It is intended to be performed Monday through Friday, during normal business hours, and while the client is using the data live. (We have documented this process in our *Network Migration Workbook*.)

Obviously, migrating a client from one set of hardware to another with zero downtime has great advantages. Most people never adopted this approach – even after buying our book. But many people told me that they learned a great deal about the strategies of ZDTM (zero downtime migration) and greatly improved their processes.

Now the very good news: It is even easier to move to cloud services with zero downtime. In fact, it's hard to have downtime at all unless you work at it!

Let's walk through it one service at a time.

Step One is planning. Make a list of all the services on the client's network and decide where you want all of them to live when you are done with the migration. For example, let's say you identify the following services within the client's operation:

- Active Directory
- Activesync
- Desktop Environment
- DHCP
- DNS (in-house)
- DNS (Internet)
- Domain Control
- Email / Exchange
- Firewall
- Internet Connection
- Line of Business (LOB)
- Online Backup
- On site Backup
- Patch Management
- Printing
- Remote Monitoring
- RWA
- SharePoint
- Spam Filter
- SQL Database(s)
- Storage (Files)
- Telephone service
- Terminal Server / Application
- Virus Protection
- VPN (if needed)
- WWW

Now simply write down the various locations or services and where they will be after you're finished with the migration. For example:

On site (with Server Lite)

- Active Directory
- Desktop Environment
- DHCP
- DNS (in-house)
- DNS (Internet)
- Domain Control
- Firewall
- Internet Connection
- On site Backup
- Printing
- RWA
- Terminal Server / Application
- VPN (if needed)

Hosted with Email Service

- Activesync
- Email / Exchange
- SharePoint
- Spam Filter

Hosted with RMM / Service Desk

- Patch Management
- Remote Monitoring
- Virus Protection

Hosted with Storage

- Online Backup
- SQL Database(s)
- Storage (Files)

Hosted Elsewhere

- Line of Business (LOB)
- Telephone Service
- WWW

Create a Network Documentation Binder (NDB) and put this information in it. This will be the beginning of documenting the new configuration. As we'll discuss, this documentation is more important than ever.

Once you start taking things apart like this, it becomes pretty easy to see how you can start moving services to the cloud one at a time. The easiest is probably the client web site. In fact, it's probably already hosted somewhere else.

Spam filtering, RMM, and patch management are probably already with you or a service you resell. So those can be checked off as well. If you provide the antivirus products, check those too.

Under the Resources section, we have a Client Onboarding Checklist and a Cloud Migration Checklist. Obviously, those are available as .docx files in the downloads that accompany this book (see instructions at the beginning of this book or browse to SMBBooks.com to find the registration link).

You'll want to fine-tune the checklists for your specific requirements and clients. In the meantime, the next four chapters dig into the practical considerations of migrating, specifically with regard to data (files and folders), email, and Microsoft Office products. Then we conclude this section of the book with more money-making homework you can do to prepare your clients for cloud services.

I think it's helpful to have one (big) client in mind as you go through this material. Most of your clients probably have similar setups simply because you have a preferred way of managing all these services already. Now you're developing your preferred cloud-centric version of the same thing.

It's also probably helpful to start jotting down some client-specific notes. These will be useful as you move into Chapter 18 and creating client-specific migration plans. Eventually, you will sit down with a client and tell them, "We've thought about what you need and we think this is your best path. This stays on site; this goes to a hosted server; this goes to a hosted service; etc."

You'll mention that you could put together a quote for a new server, but that might be $5,000 or $6,000 plus labor, and the whole deal would be close to $10,000. OR we can get you onto cloud services for about $2,500 and you'll have monthly service fees instead of a server on site.

And yes, you're committing to three years of service, but you're not going to be buying that server.

Choose the Right Partners

I like to choose larger companies to do business with, and those that are publicly traded, because they have a fiduciary responsibility to maintain that data and to maintain the financial viability of their company. Way back when we started down this road, we had a little handwritten sign in our office that read, "Rackspace has spent $7.4 billion more than we have on security."

People always worry about their data in the cloud. But no matter what a small business is willing to spend to secure a server on site, it is less secure with one access point that can be beat on day and night for the rest of eternity than a system in the cloud that's properly configured.

So, I would not resell something that a friend of mine put together in his own colo and backed up to his garage. But reselling Microsoft I have no problem with.

I have no qualms reselling Sherweb, Intermedia, Rackspace, or Amazon Web Services because they are working hard every day and every night to make sure this stuff does not break. They're some of the only ones that have true redundancy. So many people go on and on and on about redundancy and there's a tiny little asterisk that says "available for an extra price."

You want services that you know are safe, and if you're going to do HIPAA, you need to use services that will sign a business associate agreement. Those services will have a web page that tells you how you can sell these services as being secure with HIPAA.

Also, many countries have laws regulating where the data have to be stored, including Canada, Australia, and most of Europe. Even aside from that, there are industries that have further guidelines about where data can be stored and how it has to be stored (e.g., encrypted).

Bottom line: You need a service that meets those requirements.

It's important that you carefully choose the services that you resell, so that's why we're going to spend some time going through some of those services.

Alright, let's start planning our work!

Remember what we sell (see previous chapters). Our Cloud Five-Pack™ is delivered with the following services:

- Storage / Backup
- Email boxes
- Spam filtering
- Email archiving
- Email encryption
- Web site
- RMM / Patch management
- Antivirus
- Microsoft Office

Now let's re-order that list in the order we'll migration each service. My preferred order looks like this:

- Web site
- RMM / Patch management
- Antivirus
- Storage / Backup
- Email boxes
- Spam filtering
- Email archiving
- Email encryption
- Microsoft Office

First of all, if the website is still in-house, get it out-of-house as quickly as possible. That should have been done 20 years ago.

Next up: Remote monitoring and antivirus. The remote agent allows you to begin the migration process. It gives you visibility into the entire network. And, once you start patch management and monitoring, you've got a big step up on keeping the local environment under control. See Chapter 14.

Storage is very easy. And the beautiful thing is that you can move all the files and folders during the evenings so there is zero downtime. See Chapter 15.

Email is probably the most complicated thing that you have to move. I start with the spam filter because that makes everything easier. With a hosted spam filter, you can simply stop pointing to the old location and start pointing to the new. It just works. The clunky part is moving the big bulk of mailbox data up to the new cloud. But, again, no downtime. See Chapter 16.

Office is last, for me, because I have to either connect remotely or physically go to every single desktop. But when you're done with Office, it's all done. See Chapter 17.

Note on Labor: You can reduce your costs significantly by having as much of this as possible assigned to outsourced labor or to administrative assistants. There is no excuse to pay a technician $50,000 or $75,000 per year to do things that can be done by a $20/hour administrative assistant.

How Much Do You Charge for Migration to the Cloud?

I mentioned a price above of $2,500. That's a common price, but you need to be sure to determine a price that makes sense for your company and your clients. You need to create a formal project and estimate how many hours it's going to take to clean up the data and move it.

We have two pricing strategies for migrations. One is for "strangers" (new clients), and the other is for existing clients. Here's why: Everyone has a closet full of crap stacked to the ceiling with things that are going to fall on you when you open the door. In other words, everyone has redundant data, undocumented databases, massive bloated mailboxes that have never been cleaned out, and so forth.

Every client has a mess you are bound to run into during the migration process. For strangers, we have no idea what the messes are or how much we'll be sidetracked by them. With existing clients, there's a much higher probability that we know where the messes are.

For new clients, I usually charge $1,500 or the equivalent of one month's managed services. I always try to keep my setup fees equal to the monthly fee. I can do that with strangers because I'm also going to have a separate cleanup project after I move them to the cloud. I'm just going to literally move everything that I can and then say, "We really need to clean up your stuff," and so there will be a separate project for that.

With existing clients, it's easier to have a project to clean up messes before we move them to the cloud. So for existing clients, we have a much clearer picture and estimate of the hours it will take. Such a project might be $2,500, for example, for 10 users.

Both (strangers and existing clients) will probably pay about the same in the end, but we simply have less knowledge about the new clients.

Note, also, that we charge a setup fee for the Server Lite. So, if the monthly charge on that is $150, then the setup fee is $150 as well. Remember that we own that server and place it at the client's office for a service fee.

My goal is to recoup my investment in the Server Lite in about ten months. And with any hardware component, such as Server Lite or a BDR, I tend to be signing a three-year deal. If there is no hardware component, then I am happy to have a contract that automatically renews month-to-month.

A Few Key Take-Aways:

1. Zero downtime migrations are easy with cloud services

2. Focus on moving one service at a time

3. Choose good, reliable vendor partners

Additional Resources to Explore

- Karl W. Palachuk and Manuel Palachuk, *Network Migration Workbook*

Notes:

14. Managed Service Tools and the Cloud

Before we dig into the specifics of migrating Storage, Email, and Office, let's take a look at all the various tools and applications you need to run your managed cloud services operations. Most of these are familiar to you.

Of course you need managed service-specific tools. These include an RMM (remote monitoring and management) and a PSA (professional services automation). One allows you to actually deploy cloud services and provide services. The other helps you run your business internally.

I don't believe this is the place to review all the options for RMM and PSA tools available today. The variety of options here grows every year. Let me just encourage you to commit to using a real, professional tool for each of these. Non-industry-specific options, and tools that don't easily integrate with every other tool out there, will end up wasting your time and money. Good, professional, name-brand tools will make money for your company.

RMM: Products Mentioned in a Recent Roadshow

Disclaimers:

- The world moves fast. Since you're reading this in a book, I'm sure some more options are available.
- A mention is not an endorsement
- There are no paid placements
- If I forgot your favorite product, please forgive me

Atera – atera.com

Autotask AEM (Datto RMM) – datto.com/business-management/datto-rmm

Auvik – www.auvik.com

AVG RMM – avg.com/ww-en/managed-workplace

Comodo – comodo.com

Continuum – continuum.net

Kabuto – repairtechsolutions.com/kabuto/

Kaseya – kaseya.com

LabTech (ConnectWise Automate) – labtechsoftware.com

Ninja RMM – ninjarmm.com

SolarWinds MSP – solarwindsmsp.com

SyncroMSP – syncromsp.com

There are some related products that are not on this list because, while they provide network monitoring, they do not perform the fundamental remote management piece that we discuss in this chapter. Some of these tools are better than others with dedicate "remote control" features. I encourage you to do some research and pick one if you do not already have one.

Luckily, most people have *something* they rely on today for remote control. If your preferred tool is robust enough to build a business on, keep it. If you're not sure, you might want to explore some other options.

RMM Is Central to Cloud Services

(and RMM is central to managed services)

On the cloud services front, the RMM tool is a key element of deploying your services and executing ongoing maintenance. I like to remind people that there's a simple way to tell whether or not someone is your client: Your client has *your* RMM agent in the lower right-hand corner of their screen!

When we get to the click-by-click of setting up a new client on cloud services, you'll see that the RMM is central to that process. Combined with Golden Hours, your RMM tool allows you to do an amazing amount of work with zero downtime during business hours.

In our *Network Migration Workbook* (2nd ed., page 81), Manuel Palachuk and I describe the concept of Golden Hours. It boils down to this: During the work day, there is one Golden Hour before the client's employees show up, one Golden Hour after they go home, and potentially a Golden Hour during lunch.

These hours are Golden because they allow you to connect to workstations, reboot services, reboot the router, and perform other disruptive tasks without causing any downtime during normal business hours.

Very often, during cloud migrations, we will have a technician come to work an hour early. He is then able to connect remotely to client machines, install our agent, apply updates, configure services, and even reboot the desktop if need be. And it's all done before the client sits down to start work at 8:00 AM.

We can do something similar at the end of the day. We just ask a technician to show up an hour later than normal and stay an hour later. In these situations, the tech only works a normal work day, so we incur no overtime. The client is not disturbed by our activities. And there's zero downtime.

As an added bonus, you may be able to kick everyone off the

network during the lunch hour during a migration project. Or, at a minimum, let them know that you reserve the right to reboot devices, repoint the firewall, etc. during the lunch hour.

Anyway, RMM is critical to deploying services. As you'll see, we prefer to connect remotely to set up a number of services and put things in place. There is no real reason for us to go on site, sit at computers, and physically touch the keyboard.

Once clients are migrated to cloud services, you will use the RMM to deploy patches and updates. And, of course, if anything goes wrong, you'll be able to connect remotely and work on their machines.

PSA: Products Mentioned in a Recent Roadshow

Disclaimers:

- The world moves fast. Since you're reading this in a book, I'm sure some more options are available.
- A mention is not an endorsement
- There are no paid placements
- If I forgot your favorite product, please forgive me

- **Autotask** – Autotask.com

- **ConnectWise** – connectwise.com

- **SolarWinds MSP** – solarwindsmsp.com

- **SyncroMSP** – syncromsp.com

- **TigerPaw** – tigerpaw.com

In addition, you'll find that many RMM tools are now morphing into an RMM/PSA combination product. Again, this is a fast-changing world. Please do some homework. But please choose something to run your business profitably.

Love Your PSA – But Make It Work for You

While a PSA is not directly related to cloud services, it is related to the smooth running of your business. If you set it up right, it's where you'll manage your employees, manage your clients, determine your profitability, and control your service board (ticketing system).

Your PSA is your LOB – Line of Business application. Just as your clients run IMIS or American Contractor or Dentrix, you need to use something to manage your entire business. That's your PSA.

The part we care about the most in this book is your ticketing system. So you might have a non-PSA ticketing system. That's fine. We're going to use PSA and ticketing system interchangeably.

In the checklists at the end of the book, we make frequent reference to creating tickets and working tickets. In the big picture, you can use whatever you want. But I highly encourage you to use a good, IT-focused, professional PSA.

Stop Whining (Whinging)

I have heard people complain about the cost of RMM tools and PSA tools. A good RMM can be had for about $1.50 USD per desktop when purchased in low volume. With higher volume, or an ASCII membership, you can get the price down from there.

So when people complain that they're paying, say $1,500 per month for their RMM, all I can think of is **good for you!** That means you have 1,000 agents deployed. In my book that's about 200 of the Cloud Five-Pack™, bringing in about $599 each, which is roughly $120,000.

If that's not what you're bringing in with 1,000 RMM agents, you're doing something very wrong. Please email me and we can set up a phone call. Email karlp@smallbizthoughts.com. I'm not kidding.

An RMM agent, properly deployed and invoiced, is the single greatest money-making tool you have in a managed service/cloud service business. Never complain about the cost. When that number gets big, your revenue better be a lot bigger.

Your PSA is almost the same story. Yes, it *is* a lot more expensive. But it should also more than pay for itself. Remember that one of the most important jobs of a PSA is to **track your time**. That's harder than it sounds, but critically important.

Tracking your time means: 1) Track 100% of your tech time for 40 hours each week; 2) Use your PSA to determine payroll; 3) Use your PSA ticketing system to determine the profitability of clients; and 4) Use the PSA to invoice clients.

In order to make all that work, you have to fully implement the time tracking options, the ticketing system, the payroll options, and the integration with your financial systems. There's a lot of work involved. But when it's done, your PSA will pay for itself every month. Guaranteed.

I used to joke that the most expensive things in my life were my house, my car, and my PSA. Then it became my house, my PSA, and my car. (PSAs are a lot cheaper than they used to be.) But it was still worth it because I saved more money with my PSA than I spent on it.

Oops. I managed to climb up on another soapbox. So I'll climb down now. But the bottom line is simple. It costs money to be in business. This is your business. Invest in good tools.

I never worked fast food. My high school job was working at the local hardware store - Roy's Hardware in Yakima, WA.

There were a bunch of old guys who would wander in every day and then Dave (the owner) would go off to have coffee with them. They all bragged about how good they were with carpentry, plumbing, etc.

But I sold them their tools. And I could always tell what grade of tools each of them would buy. The guys whose hands were most busted up and abused always bought the second-rate tools. And, often, they refused to buy the right tool for the job because it cost too much.

The guys who bought the best tools ended up busting their knuckles a lot less. They bled less, broke fewer fingers, and made enough money to buy the good tools.

I learned that good tools are an investment in my business.

A Few Key Take-Aways:

1. You need a good, professional RMM tool

2. You need a good, professional PSA tool

3. Don't whine about the cost of these things. They make you a lot of money!

Additional Resources to Explore

- **Atera** – atera.com

- **Autotask AEM** (Datto RMM) – datto.com/business-management/datto-rmm

- **Autotask (PSA)** – Autotask.com

- **Auvik** – www.auvik.com

- **AVG RMM** – avg.com/ww-en/managed-workplace

- **Comodo** – comodo.com

- **ConnectWise** – connectwise.com

- **Continuum** – continuum.net

- **Kabuto** – repairtechsolutions.com/kabuto/

- **Kaseya** – kaseya.com

- **LabTech** (ConnectWise Automate) – labtechsoftware.com

- **Ninja RMM** – ninjarmm.com

- **SolarWinds MSP** – solarwindsmsp.com

- **SyncroMSP** – syncromsp.com

- **TigerPaw** – tigerpaw.com

15. Storage Migration

Are you ready to move data to the cloud?

Let's do it!

This chapter is all about getting your client's data off the server and into the cloud – with zero downtime. Okay, you're suspicious of that ZDTM (zero downtime migration) claim. But you'll see how easy it is right away.

The basic process looks like this:

1. Configure the cloud storage. That is, buy it, set it up, define how much you need, how you access, security, etc. All that is a lot easier than it sounds.

2. Create scripts to copy all client data into the hosted storage. This is done at night when no one is using the data, and can take as long as it needs to.

3. On migration day, you move people OFF the server data store and ON to the cloud storage. From now on, all work is done on the cloud-based storage.

4. Set up a "backup" to copy the data back down to a local device every night.

When you're done with all this, the client's live data is in the cloud and the backup is on your local device – such as a Server Lite.

Note that this migration process can take days, weeks, or months. It doesn't matter because each stage is distinct and only one of them actually affects any users (step #3).

Before that, you're just creating a storage area and copying data. The client doesn't need to be involved and they are not affected in any way. After that, the client just uses the cloud storage and you manage the backup. Again, they don't know or care about what you're up to – as long as their stuff works.

Side Bar: Ransomware and Cloud Storage

I have been using some combination of Jungle Disk, Amazon Web Services, and Rackspace for more than twelve years as I write this. I have never seen these systems affected by ransomware of any kind.

Having said that, PLEASE don't think your clients will be immune from ransomware or other viruses. The services do everything they can to avoid such problems. But the bad guys grow smarter and trickier every day. And as the worlds of machine learning and artificial intelligence get smarter, the danger continues to be real.

Almost any service you use (those already mentioned, plus Azure, eFolder, and others) will have documents and instructions to make sure you are HIPAA compliant, GDPR compliant, SOX compliant, etc.

But none of them can promise that you are immune from bad things such as ransomware. Just because your data is stored in an encrypted format does not mean that it cannot be further encrypted. The end user will have the ability to read and write to this data source. Therefore, these services cannot stop somebody from encrypting these folders within the encrypted folders.

You (meaning *you*, not the client) must be responsible for creating a backup scheme to protect this data. See the chapters in the next section. Whether you rely on version control, offline files, BDR, or something else, you have to make sure you can recover all data in a timely manner when disaster strikes.

As I write this, there was a story in the news this morning about a city government whose data was encrypted. But that probably doesn't help you figure out when I wrote this because it happens all the time.

Now more than ever in the history of our industry, you must protect your client's data. More often than not, you are protecting the client from themselves. But it doesn't matter. You are taking their money month after month, and there is no excuse for losing data from an attack that is 100% predictable.

Pick Your Storage Flavor

The 800-pound gorillas for online storage are AWS (Amazon Web Services), Azure, IBM, Google, and Alibaba. But there are dozens (well, hundreds) of other providers. Many of them are simply reselling the largest providers.

You have to find a partner who is reasonably priced, works well with your chosen tools, and provides absolutely reliable storage.

Note: I am a HUGE fan of having a mapped drive letter. At least for the next five years, you are guaranteed that clients will be familiar with the concept of a drive letter versus a UNC (universal naming convention). Plus, older software often requires a drive letter. In fact, many programs that claim to work with UNCs don't.

I'm going to use the example of Jungle Disk mapping a drive letter to cloud storage. As of 2019, Jungle Disk works with your AWS account, Rackspace, or Google Drive. I suspect you will see more connections going forward.

I personally like Jungle Disk because it has very powerful caching and versioning built in. I used to use AWS for cloud storage, but moved to Rackspace as they only charge for data at rest, not for data in transit.

There are other tools that also supply a named drive letter, including eFolder's Anchor product. I did a test-drive of the Anchor product and was impressed, particularly with the granularity of their security settings. But I have not deployed this product to any clients.

In general, I like the Jungle Disk mapped drive over a "synched" local drive. As we've deployed Jungle Disk to dozens of clients (and thousands of endpoints), the cloud drive mapping works well enough that people simply open files direct from the cloud drive. The performance is excellent. Yes, there's file synching, but it is in the background and invisible to users.

Now, let's take a deep dive into the four-step process outlined at the beginning of this chapter. While our example uses a mapped drive with Jungle Disk, you can use a WebDAV or other service to map drives with other services. And to the extent that a service offers a UNC (such as OneDrive or Azure), Robocopy will work with that as well.

Recall that these are the four steps in the process:

1. Configure the cloud storage.

2. Copy all client data into the hosted storage.

3. On migration day, you move people OFF the server data store and ON to the cloud storage.

4. Set up a "backup" to copy the data back down to a local device every night.

Go do step one. That's not included in this deep dive. You will need to figure all that out and whether you'll be mapping a drive letter or using a UNC.

Deep Dive: Intro

Moving Data with Robocopy

Sample Robocopy scripts are presented in Chapter 28. Note that these are in the downloads as TXT files. Edit as needed with Notepad or your favorite text editor.

Robocopy is a truly great utility that was released with the first version of Windows Resource Kit for NT 3.5. It has been in all the resource kits since then. Now it is built into the operating system for desktops since Windows Vista and servers since 2008.

The bottom line: Robocopy is now built into pretty much any Windows operating system you're likely to use for moving data to the cloud.

Robocopy is extremely powerful. One of its primary features is to synchronize two drives. We won't really be using it for that, although you can use those switches if you wish.

In my examples, I set it up to simply copy files to the destination folder. That way, I might copy too much data, but I will never delete any. We have long used it for migrations because it will run continuously until it's successful.

If you choose to, you can set switches so that the program counts the number of changed files and then synchronizes when a specific threshold is met. In our *Network Migration Workbook*, we use those switches. But not here.

Ready? Let's execute.

Step Two: Copy the data from the old server to the new cloud storage.

Notice that I'm going to refer to the only server as the *old server*. This is primarily to make it easy to keep straight the old and the new. Old is the old server. New is the cloud storage.

Please refer to the checklist and sample script in Chapter 28 labeled *R1: Robocopy to Cloud Storage Checklist*. We're going to walk through that now.

Here's what the script looks like:

```
rem last updated karlp 20190610
rem date stamp
c:
cd \!Tech
del ~robo_e2r.bak
rename ~robo_e2r.log ~robo_e2r.bak


echo /\/\/\/\/\/\/ >> C:\!Tech\~robo_e2r.log
echo \/\/\/\/\/\/\ >> C:\!Tech\~robo_e2r.log
date /t >> C:\!Tech\~robo_e2r.log
time /t >> C:\!Tech\~robo_e2r.log


robocopy „E:\LocalDataBlob" R:\ /e /r:1 /w:1 /
mt:12 /rh:2000-0459 /log:c:\!Tech\~robo_e2r.log
echo CompanyData copied to R:\ >>
C:\!Tech\~robo_e2r.log
```

The script executes and then verifies that the working directory is **c:\!Tech**. This makes your life easy because there's only ever one place you look for log files or scripts.

For this example, the data on the old server is on drive E:

For this example, the data on the new cloud storage will be on drive R:

The command *del ~robo_e2r.bak* simply deletes the backup log file. You're going to run this job a lot, and there's no point in keeping a bunch of log files around, or letting one log file keep growing forever.

Next, we rename the .log file to a .bak. That way we can execute the script but still keep the previous log file.

We've got a couple of different log files here. The echo puts the command into the log so it's easy to see what's going on.

We're going to create a log called ~robo_e2r.log.

The E drive is on the old server. This script runs on the old server and it copies data to the R (cloud) drive in the cloud. We put some hashes and then put a date stamp in the log file. This makes it easy to find the beginning of the job.

The command that matters is

> Robocopy "E:\LocalDataBlob" R:\

That literally copies everything from the root of the local E data store to the new root of the cloud data store.

The rest of the line is a series of switches. Here's what they do:

> /e means to copy a folder even if it is empty

> /r:1 means to retry a copy one time if a file is in use

> /w:1 means to wait one second between retries

> /mt:12 means to use twelve (multi-) threads

> /rh:2000-0459 means run hours from 8PM to 5AM

> /log:c:\!Tech\~robo_e2r.log defines the log file

Later, you'll see a script that includes an /xd switch. That's exclude. We're going to exclude the directory with sensitive financial data from the Robocopy job and then run a command to move that sensitive data to a different cloud storage area.

On the wait and retry options, the default is to wait three seconds and retry forever until the sun explodes at the end of time. So never use the default.

In our situation, we're not really trying to wait until a file becomes available. You will run this job every night until all the data has been copied. So we'll wait until tomorrow and try again.

The run hours are very important. This job will start at 8:00 PM, when we assume all clients are off the system. In a perfect world, it will finish at 5:00 AM and the server will settle down and be ready for business when the client arrives at 8:00 AM.

I strongly advise that you start out with a much smaller window of operation. For example, you might run this job from 8:00 PM until midnight the first time you run it. Then, examine the log file the next day. You're going to see that the execution stopped at midnight, but the last file was written well after that.

It would be a monstrous calculation to guess how long it takes to fill the cache on the memory, the processor, the network cards, the firewall, the router, and every router between your server and the cloud storage.

When you run this job, it will consume one hundred percent of the available processor time, server memory, network bandwidth, local disc read time, etc. In other words, you will make the server essentially unusable while this job is running.

So, I recommend you start with a relatively brief run time. Then the logs will tell you how long it took between the end of the run time and when the server was actually done processing the data.

Gradually, you can increase the run hours so the job finishes a little later and then a little later. What you don't want to do is to butt up against the client's start of business (eight o'clock or whenever they show up for work).

The Robocopy log file will print out every single file in the company data folder, and whether it was successfully copied or not. It will also tell you why a copy was unsuccessful. In most cases, this would be because a file was in use. This is unlikely night after night. But it does happen.

Finally, we echo into the log file that the job is finished. Robocopy will give you a nice summary of the total files and folders copied and not copies, and why for each.

Dealing with Sensitive Data

In small business, it is very common that one or a few people have access to sensitive data that the rest of the office do not have access to. This might include payroll, personnel records, partner memos, etc.

There are various ways to separate this data so it is secure. Here's a way to do this with Robocopy. Basically, we exclude it from the job above and then copy the data to a new place. In this example, sensitive data is in the folder "E:\LocalDataBlob\Finance\bwdata" – so we exclude that from the previous command.

Now the Robocopy command looks like this (all one line):

```
robocopy "E:\LocalDataBlob" R:\ /xd "E:\
LocalDataBlob\Finance\bwdata" /e /r:1 /w:1 /
mt:12 /rh:2000-0459 /log:c:\!Tech\~robo_e2r.log
```

Then we create a new cloud storage area and map it to drive M: (for money). And we add a new Robocopy command that reads

```
robocopy "E:\LocalDataBlob\Finance\bwdata" M:\
/e /r:1 /w:1 /mt:12 /log:c:\!Tech\~robo_e2o.log
```

Now, everyone with access to all the rest of the company data has no access to the sensitive data. In fact, they don't even see it. Remember, you don't have Windows NT permissions on the data in the cloud storage.

You can rely on the new (2019+) Microsoft Active Directory Certificate Services to secure the data. But you're going to want to make sure you take time to understand that before you deploy it and assure the client you've set it up right.

Notice that I did not use the /rh (run hours) switch here. The reason for that is that the big company store might take days to synchronize, but the core financial data or personnel records are probably pretty small. If you feel more comfortable leaving the switch in, there's no harm in that.

Running the Script

With the switches we've defined, you could enter this script interactively on the server console and it will start every night at 8:00 PM and stop itself at midnight, or whatever you specify. Then it will just sit there until 8:00 PM again.

But we don't do that. If someone closes that window for any reason, the script won't start again. Obviously, if the server is rebooted for any reason, the script won't start again.

That's why we run this script via TaskScheduler (also built into the Windows operating system). Running via TaskScheduler, the script will kick off every night as you wish and will exit the window when completed. So you're guaranteed both a start and a stop time.

There are many other file synchronizing programs and scheduling programs out there. Use what works best for you. I use these because they are universally available and excellent.

I also recommend that you create a backup user in the backup security group that is used exclusively for this job. That way, it will run even if your password or the administrator password changes for any reason.

Now let's take a quick look at

Step Three: Move users OFF the server data store and ON to the cloud storage.

Please note. In the "Client Onboarding Checklist" in Chapter 29, you will see the click-by-click instructions for this procedure.

Recap – Where we are in the process.

At this point, you have gradually moved a copy of all data into the cloud storage. It might take a few days or even a week, depending on your up-bound Internet connection.

While that's happening, you need to prepare all machines on the client network for using the cloud storage as their primary storage. This requires that you connect remotely to each desktop and install two things.

First, you will install your RMM agent. This allows you to start patching and monitoring all machines. It also makes remote access easier as you will see all machines on your dashboard.

You will need a tracking sheet or tick list for this. You cannot miss any machines. I don't recommend creating a service ticket for each machine, but that's an option as well.

Second, you will install the Jungle Disk application on each desktop. Note: If you're moving data to the cloud, Jungle Disk is already installed on the server.

As part of the installation procedure at each desktop, you configure Jungle Disk consistently across all machines (see the checklist) and then disable the service.

You disable the service so it doesn't actually run at this time. The icon never shows up, the user is never confused, and they don't have a mapped drive to the cloud. At this point, the end users have no idea that all this work is going on. It has no effect on their daily routine.

This is a perfect example of using the Golden Hours we discussed in the last chapter. For example, you can use the hours of 7:00 AM to 8:00 AM each day to connect to machines and run through the setup checklist for several machines per day. Again, you might also do the same for a number of machines in the Golden Hour of 5:00 PM to 6:00 PM.

You do need to communicate with your primary contact at the client and let her know that people need to stay off their machines before 8:00 AM and get off by 5:00 PM. Obviously, if you have a technician come in an hour early (or an hour late), they can get a lot of work done without costing you any overtime.

At some point, you have completed the setup on every desktop. At that point, you have your RMM and your Jungle Disk agents on every machine. Now you're ready to make the big switch: Stop using the local server as the primary data store and start using the cloud storage as the primary data store.

The Big Day

(Again, see the checklist for details.)

Part of your documentation should be to determine how client machines acquire their mapped drive to the server (for example, via logon batch file or group policy).

On the big day, you're going to get into the client's office early. You need to disable the group policy or autoexec.bat or whatever process maps a drive to the server. Then, you need to make sure that you disable the share on a server. That way, no one can connect by any means.

Next, you need to once again touch every desktop and start the Jungle Disk server, and set the service to start automatically. That will automatically map one or more drive letters to the cloud, depending on your setup.

Obviously, you need to test all of this.

Note also that all of this "day of" stuff can be done remotely. If there are lots of desktops, you may need to call in several techs to assist. I prefer to have at least one person on site in case something goes wrong and we need to put it all back the way it was. The on site person would then be in charge of public relations with the client.

Finally, when all the client's employees show up for work, you need to usher them all into the conference room. Tell them what's happening. The old drive "X" is gone and the new drive "Y" is in the cloud.

Tell them everything should just work. They may have shortcuts that point to the wrong drive and you can switch those around. You will be in the office for at least another hour to take care of minor issues.

Ask them to try out every single function they can think of with all of the normal software they use every day. This is intended to help them gain confidence in the new system. It will also help their system begin caching the most common files and folder they access. In the long run, everything will be just a bit faster after all the caches are primed.

Note on Drive Letters

You could, theoretically, change the drive letters in Jungle Disk so it matches their old data. But, the problem with that is that very frequently they were accessing their core data not from an old drive such as *I:\companydata\blahblahblah*. If you put 100% of your cloud storage inside of a single folder called *companydata*, you've got a very clunky cloud storage setup right from the start.

As a minor problem, you have lengthened the absolute file location of every file by twelve characters. This is unnecessary. And if you have any files that are already approaching the filename+path limit of 255 characters, you might be creating some headaches for yourself.*

Personally, I like the idea that the old system (local server) and new system (cloud storage) are different. It makes clear to everyone that you are absolutely on the new system.

Status Note: At this point, all users only access data in the cloud. You have a complete "backup" consisting of 100% of this data on the local server as of 7:00 AM on the morning of the big switch. But, of course, data begins changing immediately. So the next thing you need to do is to create a backup of new cloud storage.

As for **Step Four: Set up a backup of the new cloud storage**, please see Chapter 19 on Backup Basics.

* For the super nerds in the crowd: NTFS has a file/folder name limit of 32K, but 99% of all access is through a Windows interface with a 260 character limit or a Unix interface with a 255 character limit. Since you have no idea what people will be doing in the future, try not to build systems that routinely exceed these limits.

In some cases, for example, backup systems will throw an error when a file plus path exceeds 255 characters. Just play it safe.

A Few Key Take-Aways:

1. With Robocopy (or some other synch program), you can take as long as you want to copy data to cloud storage

2. You will set up the desktops with your RMM tool and cloud drive agent so that you have zero effect on end users

3. On the big day, you will move all client users to the new cloud storage at once

Additional Resources to Explore

- Alibaba – www.alibabacloud.com/product/oss

- Amazon Web Services – aws.amazon.com/storagegateway

- Azure –azure.microsoft.com/en-us/services/storage

- eFolder Anchor –axcient.com/products/anchor

- Google – www.google.com/drive

- IBM – www.ibm.com/cloud/storage

- Jungle Disk –jungledisk.com

- OneDrive – onedrive.live.com

- Rackspace – Rackspace.com

16. Email Migration

Just as with cloud storage, moving email to hosted services can be done completely separately from any other piece of the migration process. We have had more than one client who moved data to cloud storage and waited weeks or months to move email.

In one case, a client waited more than a year. We wanted data off the old server and we wanted to get away from the old backup system. So that was a high priority for us. But due to a series of events at the client's office, they never got around to the actual email migration for more than a year.

It's a perfect reminder of the "one service at a time" mantra. It's also a great reminder of how easy it is to execute each of these things separately without affecting the client's operation.

Once again, I'll refer you to the Client Onboarding Checklist in Chapter 29. This chapter will give an overview of the email migration process.

Please note that many service providers (e.g., Sherweb, Intermedia, etc.) will help you manage the email migration for little or no charge. There are migration tools and services as well. You should move *your company email* to your preferred hosted solution and see for yourself how easy it is. Then you can decide how much outside help you might need.

When we talk about email, we also have to include hosted spam filtering and additional email-related services. We used to buy all these separately. Today, my preference is to use whatever spam filtering, encryption, and other services are preferred by my email hosting provider.

In most cases, you simply click a web form to enable these services from your hosting provider. It makes life very easy.

Hosted Exchange Providers: Products Mentioned in a Recent Roadshow

Disclaimers:

- The world moves fast. Since you're reading this in a book, I'm sure some more options are available.
- A mention is not an endorsement
- There are no paid placements
- If I forgot your favorite product, please forgive me

We all know there are hundreds of options out there. These are some of the most-mentioned.

Hosted Email Services:

AppRiver – appriver.com

Intermedia – intermedia.net

Microsoft (direct) –office.com

Rackspace – Rackspace.com

Sherweb – sherweb.com

Hosted Spam Filtering Services:

Mailprotector – mailprotector.com

Reflexion –sophos.com/lp/reflexion.aspx

SolarWinds Mail Assure –solarwindsmsp.com/products/mail

Note: Many of these services are also available through distributors, including Ingram Micro, Synnex, D&H, and Tech Data.

Email / IMAP Synchronizing Tools:

IMAP Move –edoceo.com/creo/imap-move

IMAPsync –imapsync.lamiral.info

Aid4Mail – aid4mail.com/large-scale-email-migration

Migrating Email – with Zero Downtime

Thank goodness we live in the modern era. Exchange migrations used to be one of the biggest, baddest, worst jobs you could ever undertake. With modern versions of Outlook and Exchange, migrations have become almost trivial.

But before we downplay this too much, just remember that you need to **go slow** and take your time. If you mess up someone's email, you will have a very angry and frustrated client. Maybe even a former client!

The features that make modern migrations so much easier are the ability to open multiple mailboxes in Outlook and IMAP (the Internet Message Access Protocol) in Exchange. These features make it easy to attach a new hosted mailbox (Gmail, Office 365, or others) and move email from the old system to the new system.

IMAP is also at the heart of many archiving systems and specialty filtering services such as SaneMail (www.sanebox.com). Most email migration services you employ will be using the IMAP protocol to copy all email with zero downtime.

Of course you can still export email to PST (personal storage) files, but then you have to work around the 2GB limit per file. And while IMAP will move all your email, it will not help you migrate calendars, contacts, tasks, or public folders. You may use PST files for these, or use Outlook to connect to both the old and new user mailboxes and then copy over the data.

For purposes of this discussion, we'll assume you're moving to hosted Exchange mailboxes on an Exchange 2013, 2016, or 2019 server. Note that all providers who resell hosted Exchange mailboxes include the Outlook client as part of the email subscription. So even if you sell email without an actual O365 license, you should have access to a new version of Outlook for each end user.

The first step in migrating email is to take a good *inventory* of what needs to be moved. Which users/mailboxes need to be created on the new system? Are there existing or new distribution groups that need to be created?

For each user, which folders and sub-folders need to be copied to the new system? Which contacts, calendars, and tasks need to be copied over?

For public folders, do you need to create shared calendars or resources (such as a meeting room schedule)? Are there one or more public calendars that need to be copied over?

Let's say you end up with a list like this:

Users

- Ted
    - Email
    - Calendar
    - Contacts
    - Private Folder and all subfolders
- Janet
    - Email
    - Calendar
    - Contacts
    - Tasks

- Patrice
  - Email
  - Calendar
  - Contacts
- John
  - Email
  - Calendar
  - Contacts
  - Tasks
- Amy
  - Email
  - Calendar
  - Contacts
- Laura
  - Email
  - Calendar
  - Contacts
- Betsy
  - Email
  - Calendar
  - Contacts
- Bob
  - Email
  - Calendar
  - Contacts
- Carol
  - Email
  - Calendar
  - Contacts
- Ted
  - Email
  - Calendar
  - Contacts
- Alice
  - Email
  - Calendar
  - Contacts

- Domain Admin
  - Email

Public Folders

- Company Contacts
- Company Calendar
- Vacation Calendar
- CompanyWide (type=email)

Next, you need to turn this into a checklist or Excel spreadsheet so you can make notes about how you will migrate each of these. With a small number of users, you can simply connect to both mailboxes and copy everything over.

For most public folders, you will export to PST and import into the new system. Just make sure that you do this as late in the game as possible to get all the data. With IMAP synching tools, email will not likely be lost. But manual processes such as a PST move need to be repeated – and you have to make sure you don't create massive duplicates of everything.

The Big Move – and the Catch-Up

The migration move is surprisingly easy, no matter the size of the data store. Old-timers feared Exchange migrations because we had to move the entire Exchange Public or Private store all at once. Those days are gone.

Today, the process is simple:

1) Create the mail boxes and root public folder on the new hosted Exchange system

2) Start synchronizing. My preference, as with storage, is to do this during the evening hours so it has no effect on users or bandwidth during normal business hours.

3) Connect all users to the new mailboxes (they can be connected to both old and new)

4) Switch either the MX records or spam filter to point to the new mailboxes. At this point all new email shows up in the new box.

5) Run one final one-way synch to make sure all email from the old system gets moved to the new system

6) Disconnect each user from the old mailbox when synch is complete

Somewhere in the middle of all that, you'll need to set up and migrate all the public folders and resources.

Note once again that this can all take as long as it needs to take. At no point is it possible for clients to lose email. At no point is there end-user downtime.

When you are done, you have 100% of their email on the old server. Of course, this becomes outdated immediately. But as an absolute worst-case scenario, you could go back to it if you had to. We've never had to, but you have no idea what the future holds in store for you.

Note on the Administrator mailbox: Recall the conversation from Chapter 11. We use that Administrator email for registering hardware, software, and services. That email is important and needs to be migrated.

Note on the old server: If your old Exchange server was also the old file storage server (for example, if you're removing an old Small Business Server), you may now disable the Exchange services.

Recall our discussion of the "Server Lite" alternatives. If you take the old server and shut down unneeded services such as Exchange, RWA, and SQL, it no longer needs to be a big, beefy server. If it's not too old, you may choose to use it as your backup server, backing up data from the cloud.

Just don't let it get too old. If it's not under the original three-year warranty, I highly recommend an extended warranty.

A Few Key Take-Aways:

1. Take inventory and determine how you will move user email, calendars, contacts, etc.

2. Move your own company email first. Learn how easy it can be

3. Check out the automated tools that can help you

Additional Resources to Explore

- **Aid4Mail** – aid4mail.com/large-scale-email-migration

- **AppRiver** – appriver.com

- **IMAP Move** –edoceo.com/creo/imap-move

- **IMAPsync** –imapsync.lamiral.info

- **Intermedia** – intermedia.net

- **Mailprotector** – mailprotector.com

- **Microsoft** (direct) –office.com

- **Rackspace** – Rackspace.com

- **Reflexion** –sophos.com/lp/reflexion.aspx

- **SaneMail** – www.sanebox.com

- **Sherweb** – sherweb.com

- **SolarWinds Mail Assure** –solarwindsmsp.com/products/mail

- **On Microsoft Office 365 limits**, see: https://docs.microsoft.com/en-us/office365/servicedescriptions/exchange-online-service-description/exchange-online-limits

17. Microsoft Office

Even though this chapter is in the section on "Migrating to the Cloud," this chapter isn't really about migrating. It's about implementing the final component of your Cloud Five-Pack™: Microsoft Office.

Note, please, that you could forget all this and move people to WordPerfect or Google apps. Let me just spell out my bias at the start. I think real businesses need office products to increase productivity. They could be happy with the WordPerfect suite, but would be disappointed with the watered-down versions you get with Google apps.

Throw stones if you will, but I have built my businesses based on working with companies that are paying me at least $1,000 per month for services. They are not home users and they are not one-person shops. They can afford good tools, and they expect office products to perform amazing feats. That's what they get with Microsoft Office.

Pick Your Flavor

I'm not going to cover installing Microsoft Office. But I do want to give a few notes about options.

I avoided selling the previous incarnations of Office 365 (Microsoft Business Productivity Online Suite or BPOS) for about a decade. The primary reason was simple: Money.

We used to sell open licenses, boxed product, and OEM versions of Microsoft Office. I loved selling Office Pro Plus for about $500, of which $100 was profit.

As Microsoft tried various pricing strategies with their "partners," they managed to come up with program after another that was low- or no-profit for resellers. At one point, they were pushing a version that paid about eighteen cents per month.

At that rate, a client would have to pay their Office fees every month for forty-six years for me to earn $100. And I would have to remain the partner of record.

So we didn't sell Office 365 – until they came up with a program where

1) I can charge whatever I want, and

2) I own the client. To me, that means I collect the money.

Recall our conversation of the bundle in Section III above. It's the bundle that makes this whole program go. Including MS Office is part of the bundle. We include it because it gives us some money and it solves a few problems.

As I mentioned before, a perfect environment includes new software. The latest version of Office is de facto the most secure. It closes a lot of potential holes. It makes our clients ineligible for many viruses and ransomware attacks.

So the next question is, should I sell direct from Microsoft, go through a reseller such as Sherweb, Intermedia, Rackspace, etc., or buy through a distributor such as D&H, Ingram, or Synnex?

Personally, I prefer the other interfaces I've seen to the Microsoft CSP (Cloud Service Provider) dashboard. But I know lots of people who sell direct from Microsoft and have dialed in exactly how to make money with it.

The other advantage of resellers and distributors is that they can sell you all kinds of other services that become part of your bundle. In fact, almost everything you could think of to add to your bundle is available from resellers and distributors.

When we first started, we had to go through several different providers to create our bundle. Over time, we have been able to build a better bundle with fewer vendors involved.

The really good news for you is that the client doesn't care where you get O365. You can even change the provider in the background and they won't notice the difference.

The bottom line: Go pick the provider that you want. Pick the version of O365 you want to include. And go make a bunch of money.

Questions About O365

When I present my bundle to crowds of IT providers, I am frequently asked how we compete with Microsoft at $12.50/month. The simple answer is, we don't!

We sell our *bundle*. Yes, it includes the business version of Office. So our "wholesale" is roughly equivalent to what the client is paying IF they're buying direct.

We use the cost of other services as a selling point. "Once you sign with us, you won't have any more invoices for Office 365, antivirus, spam filtering, etc. All those costs will go away."

We encourage them to think of these various costs as helping to pay for their monthly fee. With luck, they're already buying all that stuff from us, so we just move them from one kind of billing to another.

I know that many people have sold inappropriate licenses to clients. Let's be honest, if you did that, it's your fault. But some products, such as the "essential" products that have no local installation, are junk. They should not exist and would leave a bad taste in the client's mouth.

The business edition of Office gives the client downloadable code and tracks licensing on up to five devices per user. It provides a great deal of consistency for the client – and for us.

I highly encourage you to include the business class version of Office 365 in your bundle, get rid of whatever other licensing the client has, and just move forward.

A Few Key Take-Aways:

1. Microsoft Office 365 is the gold standard

2. You should be including the business grade edition of O365 in your bundle

3. If clients say they already have Office or other pieces of your bundle, use this as a sales technique

Additional Resources to Explore

- **AppRiver** – appriver.com

- **Intermedia** – intermedia.net

- **Microsoft** (direct) –office.com

- **Rackspace** – Rackspace.com

- **Sherweb** – sherweb.com

18. Money-Making Homework - Migration Plans

Ready to make some money? Good! This chapter provides you with more "homework" to start planning client cloud migrations.

The basic form for this is included in the downloads that accompany this book. Register your book at www.smbbooks.com.

Here's what we're up to: For each of your current clients, evaluate all current services and determine how and when you will move them to the cloud.

I know there's a LOT of stuff here, but you just need to fill in enough notes to figure out how you'll move this client to cloud services.

After you complete this form, you need to make notes about what the future configuration will look like. For both yourself and your client, a Visio-type diagram may be helpful.

Just as you did with storage and email, you need to take stock of what you have now so you can start making plans. You need to figure out where everything is going to be in the future.

Remember: Moving to Cloud Services is inevitable, but that does NOT mean it all has to be done at once. The client may have a new server. Their line of business application may not have a good *enough* hosted version.

There are many reasons why you might move one service at a time as it makes sense. Some elements listed here (e.g., spam filtering) are already included in your Cloud Five-Pack™. Others (e.g., Internet DNS) have to remain on site for the foreseeable future.

Some items you discover with the list will be moved this year, some next year, and some in five years. But you will be much better off to start making a plan *now*. That allows you to begin the never-ending conversation with your clients about the gradual move to cloud services.

Sample Cloud Migration Plan

Client: _____

Consultant: _____

Decision Maker: _____

Email Address: _____

Phone Number: _____

Summary: Current Setup

Primary Server: _____

Operating System: _____

Domain Controller? YES / NO

Important Software: _____

_____

_____

Primary Function(s): _____

_____

_____

Total Disc Space in Use: _____

Other Notes: _____

_____

_____

Secondary Server: _____

Operating System: _____

Domain Controller? YES / NO

Important Software: _____

_____

_____

Primary Function(s): _____

_____

_____

Total Disc Space in Use: _____

Other Notes: _____

_____

_____

SAN / NAS or other on site storage: _____

_____

Total Disc Space in Use: _____

DHCP

Served from the firewall or router

Served from Server _____

DNS

In-House (domain) is served from Server _____

_____

Internet domain DNS is:

☐ Served from in-house Server _____

☐ Hosted with Registrar _____

☐ Hosted with Web or Email Hosting Service _____

_____

Email

Exchange or basic Pop3 (circle one)

In-house on server _____

Hosted Server at: _____

Hosted Mailboxes at: _____

In-House Spam Filter: _____

Brand: _____

Model Info: _____

Other Notes: _____

Hosted Spam Filter: _____

Brand: _____

[Purchased direct by client] or [purchased through a consultant]? Circle one.

Other Notes: _____

Internet

Provider: _____

Type of Service (e.g., cable, DSL): _____

Speed of Service: _____

Line of Business Application

Name: _____

Version: _____

Housed on Server _____

Is there a Hosted version available?   YES / NO (circle one)

Backup

In-House Backup Hardware: _____

In-House Backup Software: _____

BDR Device: _____

Cloud-Based Backup: _____

Backup Size, Server One: _____

Backup Size, Server Two: _____

Other Notes: _____

Remote Access

How many users connect remotely? _____

What are they accessing? (desktop, terminal server, etc.) _____

_____

_____

How do they connect? _____

_____

Other Notes: _____

_____

SharePoint

How many people access SharePoint? _____

SharePoint is on Server _____

Database size: _____

Other Notes: _____

SQL Databases

Database Name / Data Set _____

SQL Brand and Version: _____

Database is on Server _____

Database size: _____

Other Notes: _____

Database Name / Data Set _____

SQL Brand and Version: _____

Database is on Server _____

Database size: _____

Other Notes: _____

Database Name / Data Set _____

SQL Brand and Version: _____

Database is on Server _____

Database size: _____

Other Notes: _____

VPN

If client has a VPN, what is it used for? _____

_____

_____

How many people use the VPN? _____

Other Notes: _____

_____

_____

Web Services

In-house on server _____

Hosted Server at: _____

Hosted with Web or Email Hosting Service _____

_____

Virus Protection

In-House AV managed on Server _____

Cloud-Based AV: _____

Other Notes: _____

_____

_____

Remote Monitoring and Management Tool

Brand and Version: _____

Managed from in-house Server _____

Cloud-based RMM: _____

Other Notes: _____

_____

_____

Phone System

In-House Phone System: _____

Managed by (you or someone else) _____

VoIP?   YES / NO

Number of lines: _____

Other Notes: _____

_____

_____

Additional services not listed above (and notes):

_____

_____

_____

_____

_____

_____

_____

Additional Notes:

_____

_____

_____

_____

A Few Key Take-Aways:

1. Take stock of where all your clients' data and services are now

2. Begin outlining plans to move everything to cloud services – eventually

3. Begin a never-ending conversation with your clients about their eventual move to the cloud

Additional Resources to Explore

- I have nothing specific here, so I'll use this space to encourage you to check out my membership site at www. smallbizthoughts.org

Notes:

_____

_____

_____

_____

_____

_____

_____

_____

V. Backups, DR, and Continuity

19. Basic Backups

This section covers the basics of backing up data from cloud storage. You probably already have a good idea of what works for your clients, so we're going to cover two topics briefly.

In the next chapter, we'll talk about using cloud-to-cloud backups and BDR (backup and disaster recovery) devices. We'll also discuss email backup in the next chapter. In this chapter, we'll focus on a very basic backup of your cloud data by bringing it back down from the cloud to a local storage area. This might be to your Server Lite or even to a NAS device.

When you talk about backups, you always have to start with your philosophy about backups. By that I simply mean defining how often you want a complete backup and how many restore points you want. Personally, I also add a "permanent offsite storage" component.

I have managed backups for some extremely large organizations. As a result of this experience, I put a premium on backups as the single most important task we perform for clients. If every other thing we do fails, a recovery from backup will keep the client in business.

If everyone had a good, working, tested backup, there would be no ransomware. No one would pay the bad guys because they can just restore from backup. Then the bad guys would go do something else.

Here's where we are with the basic Jungle Disk setup:

In the primary cloud storage, we have set Jungle Disk to keep a minimum of three previous versions of every file and a maximum of ten previous versions of every file.

Note that this does not double or triple the size of our data store because most files are copied to the cloud and never changed after that. Only a small fraction of files ever changes. Those changed files have up to ten versions stored.

You may back up your data store to another cloud, essentially creating an image daily (or weekly or whatever). And you may choose to create a "local" copy of your data by copying it down to your server every night. If you have a Server Lite or some other device available to you, I highly encourage this basic backup.

If the machine that you are copying to has a Windows Server operating system, you can also set up Shadow Copy so you have additional restore points on the local backup machine.

Personally, I also like to remove the backup disc from the server once a year and place it in permanent offsite storage along with whatever financial records are going offsite at the end of the year. This is the client's ultimate backup, ultimate snapshot of their business, and ultimate financial record for that point in time.

Use Robocopy to Backup Data from the Cloud

Back in Chapter Fifteen we walked through the first three steps to migrating your core data to the cloud. The fourth step is to create a local backup once the cloud storage becomes the "live" data. Here it is.

(Step Four:) Set up a backup of the new cloud storage.

At this point, the cloud storage is the primary storage for all files and folders. Clients access it all day, every day. Now we're going to bring a copy back down.

This is essentially the same process we used to put the data up, but just reversed.

First, create a dedicated area for your backup. In our example, this will be D:\Backup on the server. This folder is not shared in any way. It is never directly accessed. No one can attach to it. All it does is store your backup.

Here's our new backup Robocopy script:

```
rem last updated karlp 20190610
rem date stamp
c:
cd \!Tech
del ~robo_R2D.bak
rename ~robo_R2D.log ~robo_R2D.bak


echo /\/\/\/\/\/\/ >> C:\!Tech\~robo_R2D.log
echo \/\/\/\/\/\/\ >> C:\!Tech\~robo_R2D.log
date /t >> C:\!Tech\~robo_R2D.log
time /t >> C:\!Tech\~robo_R2D.log


robocopy R:\ D:\backup /e /r:3 /w:3 /mt:12 /
log:c:\!Tech\~robo_R2D.log
echo CompanyData copied to D:\backup >>
C:\!Tech\~robo_R2D.log
```

Here's what the script is doing. As before, we create the date stamp and take care of the log management. The important command here is *Robocopy from R to D:\Backup*.

The rest of the line is a series of switches. Here's what they do:

/e means to copy a folder even if it is empty

/r:3 means to retry a copy three times if a file is in use

/w:3 means to wait three seconds between retries

/mt:12 means to use twelve (multi-) threads

/log:c:\!Tech\~robo_R2D.log defines the log file

Note that we are not using the /rh (run hours) switch. You may want to start with an /rh switch for a night or two. But remember that the client's downward connection is almost always much faster than their up-bound connection. So this Robocopy job is going to synchronize a lot faster.

You still don't want to bump up against the 8 o'clock hour. But even a 500 GB data store should be done in one evening. After that, you don't need that /rh switch because only a small number of files changes in a single day.

After decades of monitoring synch files and backups, I have a pretty good estimate of the number of files changed per day. On average, you can expect that 10-15 files per person will change in a given day. In larger companies, the average is smaller than.

Keep an eye on this to verify for yourself. There's always a limit to how many files are going to get opened in a day and changed. The first thing that Robocopy does is check to see if the file size and the date stamp are identical. If they are, the file is not copied and the log will say why.

If you have sensitive date (in Chapter Fifteen we used the example of storing this data on drive M), then you would add another Robocopy command. First create a Sensitive Data backup area, then add a command such as this:

```
robocopy M:\ D:\sensitivebackup /e /r:3 /w:3 /
mt:12 /log:c:\!Tech\~robo_R2D.log
echo Sensitive Data copied to D:\
sensitivebackup >> C:\!Tech\~robo_R2D.log
```

And that's it. Now you've got all of your data up in the cloud—that's the primary storage—and you're bringing a copy back down every night.

Note: None of this prevents you from also using a BDR to back up that data from the local server.

I know that Robocopy seems really low-tech, but it's surprisingly resilient. Jungle Disk has its own synching tool built in. You may choose to use that as well. But you have to decide how comfortable you are relying on the same tool for backup that you are using for primary data storage.

Here's a great endorsement of Jungle Disk. Remember that client that waited a year after moving to cloud storage before they moved their email to the cloud? When we said they had to move the email, the woman who runs their office said, "I will tell you, if moving to hosted email is as great as moving our storage to hosted storage, it's going to make everything in our office better."

The bottom line is: Jungle Disk just works. Robocopy just works.

That's our basic backup of the data store. In the next chapter we'll look at backing up your Exchange mail boxes and more "sophisticated" backups such as cloud-to-cloud and using a BDR solution.

A Great Philosophy: Assume the Backup is Bad

One of the best philosophies you can have when designing a backup strategy is to assume that the most recent backup is bad. In the days of tape and disc backup, it was easy to assume that the tape or disc in the server right now is unusable.

And let's assume that whatever problem you're experiencing did not show up instantly. So let's assume last night's backup is bad. Okay: What's the best way to retrieve the most data?

This approach will prepare you to look at versioning strategies, shadow copies, and restore points. It will also give you a healthy respect for rotating backup media.

A Few Key Take-Aways:

1. Robocopy is a great tool for backing up files and folders from cloud storage

2. That's really it for this chapter

Additional Resources to Explore

- I have nothing amazing to add here. So I'll encourage you to follow my blog at https://blog.smallbizthoughts.com

Notes:

20. Cloud and BDR Backups

While we use backups to get a point-in-time snapshot of a business, the real value is in *restoring data*. In the last chapter I mentioned how important backups are. But let me be extremely clear: The absolutely most important thing we do for our clients is to *restore data* from backup.

That's why testing backups absolutely must be part of your monthly maintenance – whether the data are on site or in a cloud. This holds true with all services. Just because your data is in the cloud does not mean it is backed up. And just because it's backed up does not mean the backup is working!

Practicing monthly restores from backup provides two valuable services. First, you know for a fact that the backup is working. Second, you and your technicians have non-emergency experience restoring from backup. This is vital when an actual emergency happens.

In this chapter, we're going to give a quick overview of three backup options you should explore: Email backups, cloud-to-cloud backups, and BDRs.

You Gotta Backup Your Email!

One of the oddest assumptions in modern technology consulting is that cloud-based email is somehow "safe" and doesn't need to be backed up. I cannot imagine where this idea came from.

I suppose that the concept of "set it and forget it" from Chapter One plays a role. Like voicemail, we expect email to just be there all the time, with no additional effort.

But as a technician, you need to peek behind the curtains and ask, "Where is this email, really?" Well, it's really on a big server somewhere, in a data center somewhere. It may or may not be properly maintained. It may or may not be backed up, protected from floods, and mirrored in another cloud.

If something goes wrong on that server, someone will probably have the job of doing the best they can to restore that server. But you have to assume that their "best effort" is not necessarily good enough to guarantee that *your* mailboxes are completely recovered.

Assuming that we're using Office 365 or some other flavor of hosted Exchange mailboxes, you do not have an option to image the server. But you certainly do have the option of backing up all the mailboxes and other Exchange folders inside your email domain.

Some resellers provide a more-or-less built in mechanism for backing up the Exchange mailbox data. For example, Sherweb has a process for backing up and restoring the Exchange data if there's a problem (see https://support.sherweb.com/Faqs/Show/how-to-restore-an-office-365-mailbox-using-online-backup-new).

But many resellers do not provide easy, reliable backup strategies. So, you need to use some other system for backups. You can Google more options, but here are a few.

Exchange Mailbox Backups: Products My Clients Have Used

Disclaimers:

- The world moves fast. Since you're reading this in a book, I'm sure some more options are available.
- A mention is not an endorsement
- There are no paid placements
- If I forgot your favorite product, please forgive me

- **Backup Assist** – backupassist.com/news/exchange-individual-mailbox-backup-and-restore.html

- **Backupify** – from Datto – backupify.com

- **Carbonite** –carbonite.com

- **iDrive** –idrive.com/office-365-mailbox-backup/

- **Skykick** – skykick.com

- **SolarWinds Backup** – www.solarwindsmsp.com

- **Veeam** –veeam.com/backup-microsoft-office-365.html

You must, of course, implement your solution, document it, and create a procedure to test it, and train your staff. I'm a big believer in cross-training all your technicians so that anyone can restore a client's data when necessary. That's why we rotate all technicians through all clients to perform monthly maintenance.

Cloud-to-Cloud Backups

When you look at cloud storage options (see Chapter Fifteen), some of them are really storage plus backup, such as Jungle Disk. Others may be storage plus BDR, such as Datto.

You might think the world has just a few variations of products, but you would be wrong. It's actually amazing how different some of these products are.

You need to understand exactly what your storage and backup products are doing. After all, you need to deploy something that actually works. Understanding goes a long way to making sure it works.

Remember: For the Cloud Five-Pack™ as described here, you are

NOT backing up virtual machines. Your data exist in a data store on AWS, Rackspace, Google Drive, or someplace similar. You may also need to backup VMs (virtual machines), but the core data for most clients will not be inside a virtual server. It will be in a storage space that is provided as a service.

It is important that you understand where the backup provider is storing this data. After all, if your AWS storage has a problem, and your backup provider is also on the same service, you may have some real trouble. I think it's a good practice to back up to a different platform from the primary data store.

Here are a few options.

Cloud to Cloud Backups: Products My Clients Have Used

Disclaimers:

- The world moves fast. Since you're reading this in a book, I'm sure some more options are available.
- A mention is not an endorsement
- There are no paid placements
- If I forgot your favorite product, please forgive me

- **Azure** – azure.microsoft.com

- **Backupify** – from Datto – backupify.com

- **Barracuda MSP** –barracudamsp.com

- **Cloudberry** – cloudberrylab.com

- **SolarWinds Backup** – www.solarwindsmsp.com

- **Storagecraft** – storagecraft.com/products/cloud-backup

Repeat: You must, of course, implement your solution, document it, and create a procedure to test it, and train your staff. I'm a big believer in cross-training all your technicians so that anyone can restore a client's data when necessary. That's why we rotate all technicians through all clients to perform monthly maintenance.

BDR Backup

BDR – backup and data recovery – devices are almost the miracle product of the last ten years. At the turn of the last century, it could cost millions of dollars to create a realtime system-imaging solution. Today, this business-saving technology is available for a few hundred dollars per month.

Originally, BDR devices were boxes took images of the server they were sitting next to. Some allow you to spin up that image and use it as a live server in case of emergencies. In reality, the most common use is to spin up the virtual machine and copy over data that some idiot deleted by accident.

Still: Amazing technology.

Today, many BDRs allow you to backup virtual machines, including VMs that exist in hosted services such as Amazon, Google, and Azure.

If you have a straight forward files-and-folders cloud storage and bring a copy down every night to your Server Lite, as described above, then you may not need a BDR. After all, if that Server Lite dies, you can replace it and get a good backup the next night.

But remember that many clients will be in a hybrid environment for at least five more years. That means you will have additional servers on site. And when those servers get moved to hosted VMs, they will still need to be backed up. So while the nature of your BDR backup will change, you'll probably be using one for quite some time.

Gradually, you'll move to more VMs in the cloud replacing

physical servers on site. Then you'll move to eliminating those VMs altogether and replacing them with hosted services. One way or another, you'll need to backup the data even if the servers no longer exist.

Note: I'm not a fan of backing up desktop machines. I know many people use this as a way to deal with ransomware and other problems. We just never have.

Unless you want to dedicate a lot of resources to daily images of all machines, the machine you restore will be out of date. So you'll need to upgrade software and the operating system as soon as you restore the image.

In my opinion, that's not worthwhile. But if it's something you do, then you may have a BDR in the client's office for a long time to come.

Some Popular BDR Solutions in the SMB Space

Disclaimers:

- The world moves fast. Since you're reading this in a book, I'm sure some more options are available.
- A mention is not an endorsement
- There are no paid placements
- If I forgot your favorite product, please forgive me

- **Acronis** – www.Acronis.com

- **Axcient** – www.axcient.com

- **Azure** – azure.microsoft.com

- **Backup Assist** – backupassist.com/news/exchange-individual-mailbox-backup-and-restore.html

- **Backupify** – from Datto – backupify.com

- **Barracuda MSP** –barracudamsp.com

- **Carbonite** –carbonite.com

- **Cloudberry** – cloudberrylab.com

- **Datto** – datto.com

- **eFolder** – efolder.net

- **iDrive** –idrive.com/office-365-mailbox-backup/

- **Skykick** – skykick.com

- **SolarWinds Backup** – www.solarwindsmsp.com

- **Storagecraft** – storagecraft.com

- **Veeam** –veeam.com/backup-microsoft-office-365.html

A Few Key Take-Aways:

1. The Bottom Line: You must implement your solution, document it, and create a procedure to test it, and train your staff.

2. Just because your clients' data is in the cloud doesn't mean you don't need to back it up

3. Restoring from backups is the single most important thing we do in our business

Additional Resources to Explore

- **Acronis** – www.Acronis.com

- **Axcient** – www.axcient.com

- **Azure** – azure.microsoft.com

- **Backup Assist** – backupassist.com/news/exchange-individual-mailbox-backup-and-restore.html

- **Backupify** – from Datto – backupify.com

- **Barracuda MSP** –barracudamsp.com

- **Carbonite** –carbonite.com

- **Cloudberry** – cloudberrylab.com

- **Datto** – datto.com

- **eFolder** – efolder.net

- **iDrive** –idrive.com/office-365-mailbox-backup/

- **Skykick** – skykick.com

- **Sherweb** – https://support.sherweb.com/Faqs/Show/how-to-restore-an-office-365-mailbox-using-online-backup-new

- **SolarWinds Backup** – www.solarwindsmsp.com

- **Storagecraft** – storagecraft.com/products/cloud-backup

- **Veeam** –veeam.com/backup-microsoft-office-365.html

21. Business Continuity

Way back in the dark ages (1990s), I designed and executed disaster recovery plans for large installations. Very often the hardware and software were in the range of $500,000 per site. The disaster recovery plan literally included a list of every single piece of equipment that needed to be replaced.

On the "big iron" side, this made sense. We needed one HP-3000 mini with MPEx operating system and modules for Cobol, etc. But on the small end, we listed individual terminal screens and PCs.

Today, we have an evolved sense of what disaster recovery means. If I lost a server, I don't really need to replace that server. I need the data. And I probably need the Active Directory. But I don't need the actual server.

I might take an image and restore to a new server, to a virtual server in my office, or to a virtual server in some cloud somewhere.

. . . Or I might just realize that the whole concept that technology centers around a server is no longer accurate. I need the data, not the server.

From time to time I make a statement that irritates many people:

If your business consists of building servers and putting them in people's offices, you are operating with a business model that no longer exists.

I believe that. That model came into existence in the 1990s and died in the late 2010s.

Hosted storage and hosted email/office products are absolutely reliable today. They have been for years. So we need to focus on what works going forward.

The way I see small business technology, you have three primary options:

1. In-house physical (and virtual) servers

These systems are typified by the following attributes:

- They have a limited lifetime. I say three years. Some people say as much as five.

- They require maintenance labor. Labor = you spending your most limited resource in exchange for money.

- If they are attacked, you must defend them. And if they are destroyed you must rebuild them.

- If anything goes wrong with the client's network infrastructure, they are probably unavailable. To the client this means downtime, even if the server is actually up.

2. Hosted (cloud) virtual servers

These systems are typified by the following attributes:

- The underlying technology is physical and someone has to maintain it. When they move to new technology, you may have minor hassles. But you don't care about the physical machine.

- They require maintenance labor. Labor = you spending your most limited resource in exchange for money. Granted, you don't maintain the physical, but you must maintain the virtual machines (operating systems and software).

- If they are attacked, you must defend them. And if they are destroyed you must rebuild them.

- If anything goes wrong with the client's network infrastructure, the servers continue operating. By providing the client with alternative means of accessing the Internet, they continue to be able to access their servers.

3. Hosted (cloud) services

These systems are typified by the following attributes:

- As long as you pay the bill, it works.

- They require no maintenance labor on your part.

- If they are attacked, there's nothing you can do. The service provider is responsible for defense and security.

- If anything goes wrong with the client's network infrastructure, the services continue operating. By providing the client with alternative means of accessing the Internet, they continue to be able to access their servers.

These basically go from most expensive and fragile to least expensive and fragile.

They also go from least profitable to most profitable, based on top-line revenue.

It is critical that you stop thinking in terms of a server-centric world. "Downtime" should not rely on any specific piece of hardware (or software) failing. Downtime in the modern era means the client cannot reach their email or cannot open a file.

Twenty years ago, business continuity consisted of getting new hardware, replacing all the software, rebuilding the systems, installing all the software, restoring from backup, and putting the client back in business. If you were good and lucky, the client lost very little data.

Ten years ago, business continuity consisted of spinning up a VM on a BDR and pointing the client to that. Then, after the client was back in business, you had to get new hardware, replace all the software, rebuild the systems, install all the software, and move the VM back from the BDR to the "real" server. If you were good and lucky, the client lost no data.

Today, business continuity means that the services never fail. If the client's Internet has a problem, you need to fix that. But the services never stop working. The data never stops being available.

Remember Superstorm Sandy (Chapter Five): Everyone whose entire business was in the cloud had zero downtime. Everyone who had mission critical servers on site was down. Period. The lesson from Superstorm Sandy is: The cloud is reliable enough to bet your entire business on. And that was 2012.

Stop selling new stuff the old way.

Please see the final thoughts in Chapter Twenty-Six. Business continuity must always be center to your job. Servers should not be.

A Few Key Take-Aways:

1. Business continuity does not mean replacing the old equipment with newer versions of the old equipment

2. Hosted servers are more profitable than physical servers; hosted services are more profitable than hosted servers

3. Stop selling new stuff the old way!

Additional Resources to Explore

- Nothing comes to mind, specifically, so I encourage you to visit my SOPFriday.com site. You'll find links to hundreds of articles and videos – all focused on Standard Operating Procedures for SMB IT consultants.

VI. Running Your New CSP Business

22. The Right Partners for the Job

We covered the tools you need to actually run your company in Chapter Fourteen. Here we're going to take a "big picture" look at the kinds of tools and services you may offer.

If you've been in this business very long, you probably have some preferred partners for each of these services. But it never hurts to look at some alternatives.

As you move from providing cloud services as a *piece* of your business to providing them as your *primary* business, you will need to make sure you use a good collection of tools and services.

In all cases, it's important that you verify where these companies are located, where they store data, and whether or not they are compliant with various regulations you need to follow. Also, if you need to comply with HIPAA, you should make sure these companies have a way to sign a business associate agreement (BAA).

Also consider having two primary partners for each of these (see the next chapter on building your catalog of services). It is always good to have an alternative ready without having to do research instantly.

Below is a series of resource lists. This is not a complete list of all possible providers. It's not the ultimate list or even a "best of" list. It's just some resources that my clients have mentioned they use.

Of course, in our ever-changing world, some of these services may be combined, renamed, or gone by the time you read this. But it's a place to start.

Partner Resources for Running Your Cloud Service Business

Disclaimers:

- The world moves fast. Since you're reading this in a book, I'm sure some more options are available.
- A mention is not an endorsement
- There are no paid placements
- If I forgot your favorite product, please forgive me

Domain Registrars

- **Amazon** - aws.amazon.com

- **Direct NIC** - DirectNIC.com

- **GoDaddy** - godaddy.com

- **Network Solutions** - networksolutions.com

- **Register.com** -register.com

- **SRS Plus** - srsplus.com

DNS Providers

- Also: Your domain registrar and your web hosting provider

- **Amazon Route 53** - aws.amazon.com/route53

- **Cisco Umbrella** - umbrella.cisco.com

- **DNS Filter** - DNSfilter.com

- **DNS Made Easy** - DNSMadeEasy.com

- **Open DNS** - opendns.com

Web Hosting Service

- **DreamHost** - dreamhost.com

- **Fat Cow** - fatcow.com

- **Hostway** - hostway.com

- **Host Gator** - hostgator.com

- **Stable Host** - stablehost.com

Antivirus

- **AVG** - avg.com

- **Bitdefender** - bitdefender.com

- **Sophos** - sophos.com

- **Vipre** - vipreantivirus.com

- **Webroot** - webroot.com

Backup and BDR

- **Amazon Web Services** - aws.amazon.com

- **Axcient** - axcient.com

- **Backup Assist** - www.backupassist.com

- **Datto** - datto.com

- **Dropbox** - dropbox.com

- **Microsoft Azure** - www.azure.com

- **StorageCraft** - storagecraft.com

- **Veeam** - www.veeam.com

- **Jungle Disk** - jungledisk.com

- **Microsoft One Drive** - live.com

Email

- **Appriver** - appriver.com

- **Intermedia** - intermedia.net

- **Microsoft O365** - products.office.com

- **Rackspace** - rackspace.com

- **Sherweb** - sherweb.com

Spam Filter

- Also your preferred email provider

- **Avast** – avast.com

- **Barracuda** - www.barracuda.com

- **Reflexion / Sophos** - reflexion.net

- **SolarWinds MSP** – solarwindsmsp.com

- **Trend Micro** - trendmicro.com

Microsoft Office Licenses

- Also your preferred distributor

- **Appriver** - appriver.com

- **Intermedia** - intermedia.net

- **Microsoft O365** - products.office.com

- **Rackspace** - rackspace.com

- **Sherweb** – sherweb.com

A Few Key Take-Aways:

1. Choose a "preferred provider" for the core services you offer

2. It's a good idea to have a preferred alternative as well

3. Research your vendor partners. Make sure they meet any requirements your clients have, especially with regard to compliance.

Additional Resources to Explore

- See all of the above

Notes:

_____

_____

_____

_____

_____

_____

_____

_____

23. Your Standard Offerings (Your Catalog of Services)

What do you sell?

I mean everything. What's the entire list of every single thing you sell? If you don't have one, it can be very helpful to start one. Because it's also a good indicator of what you *don't* sell.

I won't repeat all the resources from the previous chapters, but I highly encourage you to explore a few alternatives to what you've been doing so far.

One of the best things you can do for your business is to create your **catalog of services**. This catalog should include all the hardware, software, and services you sell. Some folks call this your sales **line card**.

It doesn't have to be fancy. You can literally print out a few pages and stick them in a small three ring binder.

Why, you ask.

There are several reasons to have a sales line card. The most important is that you should limit how many different products and services you sell. For example, my companies have always preferred HP servers, HP desktops, SonicWall firewalls (except when they were owned by Dell), Brother printers, APC UPSs, and so forth.

To be more accurate, we always preferred to have one primary offering and one alternative offering. So, to be more accurate, we sold:

- HP Servers. Or IBM if we needed an alternative.

- HP Desktops. Or Lenovo if we needed an alternative.

- SonicWall or Watchguard firewalls

- Brother or HP printers

- APC or Tripp Lite UPSs

- HP or Viewsonic monitors

For software, there are some products for which we never sold an alternative. The biggest example is operating systems and office products. We sold the latest Microsoft products for each.

Our Story on Antivirus

With other software, there are alternatives. Let me share a quick history of our choice of AV software over the years.

For the longest time, we deployed both McAfee and Symantec. Then McAfee went through a period when upgrading the engine and the definitions separately became too labor intensive.

We switched to primarily Symantec, but it evolved so that upgrading became a nightmare of reboots and downloading special scripts to remove the old version so we could reboot and install the new version.

About that time, Trend Micro came out with a managed service pricing model. So we added Trend to the mix and eventually sold it exclusively . . . until we decided to deploy whatever came with our RMM agent.

Today I cannot tell you the brand name of the AV on my computer. It's whatever gets deployed with SolarWinds. And if they change, I'll change.

I tell this story because it illustrates the evolution of our relationship with several vendors, and the AV market generally. At no point did we sell "every" product out there. We sold one or two products at a time.

The Benefits of Limiting Your Options

This habit – selling one or two brands for each product line – has served us very well over the years. It brings several benefits.

1. Specialization

Selling one or two brands for each product line allows us to develop a certain level of specialization. And this applies to the line as a whole, not just to specific products. For example, there is a way that you order HP parts that is very different from Lenovo or Dell. There is a way that Brother printer software updates are different from Epson.

2. Learning and Teaching

When we limit our choices to one or two brands, it becomes easier for us to train our technicians. And, of course, that makes it easier for us to train our clients.

You cannot learn all the processes, web sites, and oddities of every product and every brand. But you can learn some! And within any brand, there are always little things that are different from other brands.

3. Documenting

We are fanatical about documentation. Whether it's "our way" of setting up a firewall or configuring a workgroup printer, we try to develop and document the process. This allows us to create consistent processes internally, and to provide a consistent experience for the client.

It would be futile to attempt a high level of custom documentation for every product and every brand out there. But documenting one or two brands is very manageable.

4. Relationships

When we limit the number of vendors, we also increase our sales of those limited vendor brands compared to all others. If we're lucky, this will lead to higher partnership levels and better margins.

For some big, nameless, faceless companies, the best we can hope for is to make enough sales to get to the next level of discounts. But for other companies with good channel programs, we can actually build personal relationships with our vendors.

Building vendor relationships can lead to increased marketing development funds (MDF), sales leads, and overall higher engagement. With selected partners, we have even been able to create client-facing events and had the vendor send speakers.

5. Selling Products

When a client says, "Please get me a quote for a new [firewall] [BDR] [laptop]," we don't have to start with Google. We don't open the search to every product on earth. We look at the brands we sell.

Plus, since we have some familiarity with the brand, we are likely to narrow down the options very quickly. With printers, for example, we have a preferred workgroup printer and a preferred personal printer for each of our two brand names. So, we have four immediate options to choose from – not hundreds or thousands.

Perhaps the single greatest way that we make money by limiting our options is by saving time when we have to prepare a quote for a client. Starting from scratch can be extremely time consuming.

6. Training Sales People

When you have sales people (even one person who is taking over for the owner), it is much easier to train them when you have a limited number of options – and they're listed in a binder.

Of course it will take a new sales person some time to learn your products and services. But that time is limited because your options are not infinite.

Note: Two options is better than three options for all the reasons above. But two options is also better than one option. With one option, you have *no options* if something goes wrong.

For example, if HP has a supply problem and you just can't get a laptop, it helps a lot if you know you'll be selling a Lenovo instead. You still have to do some research, but you're not starting from scratch, looking at every family of laptops out there.

Where to Start

To start building your line card, first determine what you sold in the last twelve months. If you use QuickBooks, you should be able to run a report of Sales by Item / Detail. That will give you a printout of everything you've sold – to the extent you put that information in the system in the first place.

Again, brands are more important than specific SKUs (stock keeping units). For example, "APC UPS" is the most important category to list. If you choose to separate desktop grade (e.g, 350 and 750) from server grade (e.g., 3,000VA), that's fine as well.

Don't worry too much about Back-UPS 350 vs. Smart-UPS 350 or listing BK350x545, BK350EIX545, BE350G, etc.

For your line card, you need to know that you sell *this brand* or *that brand* of desktop UPSs and *this brand* or *that brand* of server grade UPSs. Think about how you would train someone to take over the ordering process. Two brands maximum. A small family of options.

Note also that you should have two distributor options. In the Sample Line Card below, we note your preferred source. This is particularly true of hardware and software. If one distributor is out, or very high priced on a specific item, it's great to just order from the other distributor.

For two decades, we had two preferred distributors. We tried to divide our sales between them. This did limit our overall sales numbers with each distributor. But when we had a dispute, we simply ordered everything from the other vendor.

On two different occasions, this technique got us some needed attention. In one case, we were having no luck with the customer service department for over a month. We stopped all purchases from that distributor.

When our monthly spend dropped about $30,000 all at once, we got a call from our sales rep. "What's up?" I'm glad you asked! The problem got sorted out in less than a week.

You can't do that if you only have one distributor.

Changing Your Line Card

Our industry changes all the time. Even if you try to stick with one brand, the specific options change at least once per year. For some products, it's every few months.

Specific model numbers are far less important than brand names. If you choose Viewsonic for monitors, for example, the specific models come and go. But the model numbers follow a pattern that can tell you a great deal about the technology behind the model number.

This is a perfect example of how the brand "limitation" can increase your efficiency. When you combine this knowledge with the limitations of size and budget, there may be only a couple of options to choose from.

When you change brands, that's a much bigger deal. I highly encourage you to do some serious research before changing your preferred brands.

This research should include more than simply the approval ratings on "comparison" web sites. Call their support line on Saturday evening. Talk to other IT providers who resell that brand. Find out what their buying options are. (For example, do you need approval? Do your preferred distributors carry this brand?)

I would recommend three rules about changing brands. First, do it very slowly, with lots of research. Second, don't change too often. Third, review all choices from time to time.

I have a very good friend who always seems to be trying new things. I think he sold at least six different firewall brands one year. In each case, he talked to them at a conference, like their story, and signed up. Then he sold one to a client. If the experience was good, he sold it to other clients.

Then he went to a different conference and met another vendor.

If all the products are good, there's nothing particularly wrong with this approach. But, as you can imagine, he now has many brands deployed. He has less expertise in each one. And he has no real relationship with any of the vendors. After all, he may have sold five units all at once, but he has no track record of building a relationship.

You do need to review all relationships – even the best ones – from time to time. Don't let your line card get stale.

Obviously, if you have been selling the same brand of laptop for five or ten years, you are heavily biased toward that. There's no problem with that. But you should verify that they are progressing with the times, continuing to have a good partner program, and still a choice you would make today.

Draft Sales Line Card

The downloads for this book (register at SMBBooks.com) include a Draft Sales Line Card. This is a very simple document, but a place to start documenting what you sell.

It looks like this:

Sales Line Card

Your Name: _____

Your Company: _____

Distributors

This is the official list of your preferred distributors. This list used to be just for hardware and software. Today it can include many cloud services as well.

Primary preferred distributor: _____

Secondary preferred distributor: _____

Other distributor: _____

Other distributor: _____

Services

This is the official list of what you sell in the category of Services. List everything you sell in the categories of "hosted" or cloud services.

Do not list every single SKU you sell. Do list categories broad enough to be descriptive. For example:

- Hosted Exchange
- Hosted SharePoint
- Spam Filtering
- Backup
- Disaster Recovery / Failover

Document the Product / Brand, Current SKU, and Preferred Source(s). For example,

Hosted Exchange – Sherweb – O365 – Sherweb.com

Hosted Servers: _____

Hosted Workstations: _____

Hosted Exchange Servers: _____

Hosted Exchange Mailboxes: _____

Hosted Spam Filter: _____

Cloud Backup: _____

Cloud Disaster Recovery / Failover: _____

Cloud Antivirus: _____

Hosted Content Filtering: _____

Hosted Office Suite: _____

Hosted Creative Suite: _____

Hosted Password Vault: _____

Specialty Line of Business Application: _____

_____

Hosted SQL Server: _____

Hosted CRM: _____

Hosted SharePoint: _____

Other: _____

Other: _____

Other: _____

Hardware

This is the official list of what you sell in the category of hardware.

Do not list every single SKU you sell. Do list categories broad enough to be descriptive. For example:

- HP Servers
- HP Desktop Computers
- Brother Printers
- Watchguard Firewalls
- Datto BDR

Document the Product / Brand, Current SKU, and Preferred Source(s). For example,

HP Proliant – ABA 12345 – Ingram or Synnex

Servers: _____

Workstations: _____

Monitors: _____

Laptops: _____

Tablets: _____

Thin Clients: _____

Backup Systems: _____

Printers: _____

UPS / Battery Backup: _____

Switches: _____

Firewalls: _____

Routers: _____

BDR: _____

Memory Upgrades: _____

Network Cards: _____

Video Cards: _____

KVM switch: _____

Phones (VoIP) : _____

Cell Phones: _____

Digital Signage: _____

Security Cameras: _____

LED Products: _____

Other: _____

Other: _____

Other: _____

Software

This is the official list of what you sell in the category of Software.

Do not list every single SKU you sell. Do list categories broad enough to be descriptive. For example:

- Windows Server OS
- PDF Creator
- Microsoft Office – open licenses
- Malwarebytes Anti-Malware
- Adobe Creative Suite

Document the Product / Brand, Current SKU, and Preferred Source(s). For example,

PDF Software – PDF Forge – Ingram

Primary Server: _____

Server Lite: _____

SQL Server: _____

Email Server: _____

Other Server: _____

Other Server: _____

Other Server: _____

Office Suite: _____

Antivirus: _____

Anti-spyware Program: _____

Backup Program: _____

Defragmentation Program: _____

PDF Creator: _____

Creative Suite: _____

Financial Package: _____

Password Vault: _____

FTP Client: _____

HTML Editor: _____

Other: _____

Other: _____

Other: _____

A Few Key Take-Aways:

1. One of the best things you can do for your business is to create your catalog of services

2. Have at least two options for each – but not too many

3. Refresh your preferred options from time to time

Additional Resources to Explore

- Nothing specific to recommend here. But if you're looking for some great training, check out www.GreatLittleSeminar.com.

24. Staff Requirements for Cloud Services

When you focus on the in-house servers, the local area network, and the entire set of on-site services, you need a certain set of skills to be successful. As you move to mostly cloud-based solutions, you will need a different set of skills.

The good news – if you're the owner anyway – is that you will need fewer high-level network engineers and more administrative staff. Remember: Setting up fifty or a hundred new users on cloud services is an administrative function.

There is nothing inherently technical about setting up new accounts in Azure, AWS, Sherweb, O365, Jungle Disk, or any other service. We have had technicians do this in the past because it was a natural transition from really technical stuff to stuff that sounds technical but really isn't.

Setting up a new user on O365 with a reseller (or direct from Microsoft) can be executed flawlessly with a simple checklist. It literally consists of walking someone through a web interface. Click *here*. Enter *this* and *that*.

This work can be completed extremely efficiently by an entry level tech or an administrative assistant. It requires no knowledge of TCP/IP, networking, routing, DNS, or any other technology area.

When you examine the skillsets or knowledge areas within your company, you can see four sets of skills within SMB IT consulting. These include 1) Skills that will be critically important going forward; 2) Skills that have been and continue to be important; 3) Skills you will use less and less of in the future; and 4) Skills you will only need under very specific, uncommon situations.

I propose the following matrix of skills for each category.

1. Skills that will be critically important going forward

- Business ownership
- Business acumen generally
- Cloud-based routing, filtering, network services
- Infrastructure as a Service
- IT Consulting (big picture)
- IoT (Internet of Things) large networks
- Project Management
- Time management / Task management

2. Skills that have been and continue to be important

- Accounting software, such as MAS, QuickBooks
- Antivirus Programs
- Apple Computers / Mac OS
- Assessments of IT assets and usage, determining requirements, and making recommendations
- Backup – Basic design, configuration, testing
- Cable Internet connections
- Desktop and laptop, general skills
- Devices – Using and supporting smartphones, tablets, etc.
- Fiber Internet connections
- Line of Business Applications
- Network equipment – Switching, routing, firewall, QOS
- Remote monitoring & alert systems (e.g., SolarWinds, AEM, LabTech)
- Ticketing/Help Desk systems (e.g. ConnectWise, Autoask, SolarWinds, SyncroMSP)
- Virtualization – servers / desktops (please specify and describe)
- Microsoft Office 365
- Microsoft Produces (Outlook, Excel, Word, Access, etc.)

- Security assessments and consulting
- Wireless (802.11x)

3. Skills you will use less and less of in the future

- Active Directory setup and administration – Classic AD
- Backup software (server based)
- BDR – for in-house servers, workstations
- Citrix setup and administration
- DHCP
- DNS
- Hardware firewalls (e.g. SonicWALL, Watchguard)
- MS SQL Server setup and administration
- Network architecture design principles
- Problem solving and monitoring performance in a multiple server environment
- SharePoint implementation, and admin
- Windows Server (Planning, implementation, and administration)
- Routing
- TCP/IP protocols
- VPN

4. Skills you will only need under very specific, uncommon situations

- DSL
- Experience with different server operating platforms
- Linux planning, implementation, and administration
- MS Exchange planning, implementation, and administration
- MS Terminal Services setup and administration
- T1

Obviously, you can argue about the whole list, and any part of the list. I think you're going to find three major trends in who you need to hire in the 2020s.

First, you will need one super-star technician for every 500-1,000 endpoints. After all, DHCP, complex routing, and DNS will be with us always. But you will do less and less architecting as time goes on – and far less troubleshooting. So, while it's handy to have someone who can fix *anything*, you don't need a whole bullpen full of expensive technicians who can fix anything.

Second, you are going to be hiring more and more administrative assistants. In fact, you're going to see a whole new layer of semi-technical administrative staff who have experience with the first and second categories of above. They know enough networking and enough about administering online services to provide you with excellent service.

Third, you will need fewer staff overall. The "softer" skills of client management and customer relationships will become more and more important over time. Owners who talk to owners will be far more important than having a staff full of genius technicians who can slay any monster.

The super technical people are going to be working where the servers are – behind the scenes where you never see them. And they'll be maintaining the SQL databases and Exchange Servers. They'll be applying patches and updates to clusters of servers that you simply experience as a hosted service.

In business, we sometimes have to make decisions based on reality, even if it's not the reality we were expecting. You really need to make sure you don't continue to maintain a staff of people for the perfect 2010 consulting business.

Don't keep doing what you've been doing simply because it's what you've been doing.

And don't keep staffing the way you've been staffing just because it's the way you've been staffing.

You have to create an organizational chart and skillset matrix that serves you well today and tomorrow. And that will lead you down the road to creating job descriptions, job advertisements, and candidate evaluations based on what you need going forward.

A Few Key Take-Aways:

1. The skills you need for success will be very different as you grow a cloud-centric business

2. You probably need one super-star engineer for every 500-1,000 endpoints

3. There's an emerging class of technically proficient administrative assistants that you should be looking for

Additional Resources to Explore

-   I really have nothing to point you to here, so I'll just encourage you to subscribe to my YouTube channel at youtube.com/ smallbizthoughts

Notes:

25. Selling Cloud Services

This chapter has two parts. First, some notes on getting started with selling the Cloud Five-Pack™. Second, I give you answers to a few dozen questions you might get. If you follow the strategy outlined here, you should easily answer all these objections by the time you are talking to your larger clients and prospects.

As I mentioned earlier, I started thinking about the Cloud Five-Pack™ for super-small clients. But now I am happy to sell it to any size company. In companies over thirty users, I would have a different price structure that acknowledges they have fewer devices per user, on average.

Recall the discussion of power users in Chapter Eleven. As companies get larger, there are still only a few power users among them. You may need to adjust your per-user or per-five-pack pricing, but please note: There is no upper limit to the size of company you can sell these services to!

The first step in selling an entirely cloud-based solution is to sell yourself. Install it in your office. Move your email to the cloud. Move your files to hosted storage. Set up your backup system and your Server Lite. Own it. Live with it. Use it every day. Run your business on it.

You have to prove it to yourself. You have to make sure that you understand it, and you believe in it. It's very powerful when you look a client in the eye and say, "I run my business on the exact system we want to set up for you."

Next, you need to sell this to one of your smallest clients. Install it, deploy everything, document everything – including your processes. Then install it on more small clients.

After that, go to your next group of (slightly larger) clients. Work your way up to larger and larger clients.

As you move from clients who need one Five-pack to two Five-packs, three Five-packs, and more, you will find that you only get a limited number of questions (or objections), no matter how large they are.

As you gain real-world experience, you will be very comfortable answering all their questions based on personal experience. It is easier to answer these questions with small clients. Over time you'll realize that the answers are the same for large clients as well.

The other advantage of the small-to-large approach is that you'll have lots of practice with smaller accounts that represent a great deal of money. And you'll have all the answers practiced and polished when you get to larger clients.

You may also want to start with the clients who already have hosted line-of-business apps (LOBs). If their hosted app is already in the cloud, then you don't have to worry that they have to leave anything on site.

Many IT providers worry that those old, junky LOBs are going to keep them "on site" forever. Trust me: They won't. Eventually, one of two things will happen. Either the client will move to a hosted option, or you're going to charge them to virtualize that old server and stick it up on a cloud server. Then you're going to charge them every month for the server as well as the maintenance.

Remember: You can always move one service at a time. You can move clients to the cloud over weeks or months or years. This is where regular "roadmap" meetings come in. Talk to clients about their business.

Whether you get them to sit down once a quarter or once a year, engage them in a never-ending conversation about how their business is growing, or shrinking, changing, automating, etc. Work with them – with the assumption that you're the one who will take them to the cloud.

Because, if it's not you, it will be someone else.

Roadmap meetings allow you to have the cloud conversation in a non-sales environment. Even when you finish setting up a new on site backup, you can start the conversation of what you'll do when that backup is old. You begin laying the groundwork. You and the client decide well beforehand what to do.

And on the day that the server fails or the backup starts to give you trouble, you don't have to introduce a new topic. You just give them a quote because they've already come to the decision that they're going to make this move when that backup needs to be replaced again.

Don't Break Up the Bundle

When it comes time to start selling the Cloud Five-Pack™, I highly encourage you to *not* break up the bundle. Many consultants have said to me, "I don't know if my clients will go for that."

They will. Really.

Your clients buy Office 365 as a bundle that can be installed on up to five machines per user. (Hmmm. That sounds familiar.) They buy Netflix as a bundle. They buy bundles all the time.

One of my former coaching clients sells a three pack. I think she's leaving money on the table. I am a firm believer in not breaking up the five-pack.

But you have to believe in it. That's why you should set it up in-house and then sell it to your smallest clients. You will see how rock-solid it is.

The more that you stick to the five-at-a-time model, the better off life is. And again, it should be at a reasonable price where the client just can't argue with it.

Addressing Concerns about Cloud Services

Q. Are my files really, really always available?

A. Generally speaking, your files will be more available than with an on-site server. First, you can access the cloud service from any secure device, including a home computer, tablet, or even your smart phone. Second, there is essentially zero downtime due to maintenance. We need to verify that all the security is in place, but that's true with your current setup as well.

Q. Every time I've tried a cloud service, it was really slow.

A. I'm not sure what you've tried. We have devised a system based on bundling a set of independent services that provide excellent performance and speed. It's also flexible, so if a better solution emerges, we can transfer to that. As a rule, speed problems with cloud services are caused by one of two things: A slow system at the other end (e.g., an under-powered server) or a slow connection on your end. The best thing about cloud services is that we can always improve performance without spending money on more hardware that will be antiquated in a few years.

Q. How am I protected from a malicious employee?

A. As with any other technology solution, our cloud bundle includes a secure backup. So if files are deleted or even encrypted, we can restore from backup with very little downtime. We also have the ability to change access to the cloud services and shut out the employee very quickly.

Q. How do I know that the data are encrypted and secure?

A. We have selected well-known, reliable, first-rate services for our cloud bundle. These are companies you can depend on. We can also provide you with links to their public statements about how data are moved, stored, secured, and backed up. In reality, your data is more secure on our cloud platform than on a server in your office. You might spend $10,000-$20,000 securing your systems. Our cloud service providers spend billions of dollars on security.

Q. How exactly do you "migrate" to the cloud?

A. Our process is pretty straight forward. First, we backup your data (of course). Then we make a copy in the relevant cloud service (email, data storage, etc.). When everything is synchronized, we switch you over to the live cloud services. There are various ways to accomplish this, but our goal is also to minimize downtime – and that's easy to do with cloud services.

Q. I don't think the cloud is mature enough.

A. Cloud services are very mature. In fact, I'd argue that the cloud proved itself mature in October of 2012 when Superstorm Sandy hit the U.S. Northeast. Some areas, including parts of New York City, were without electricity for two weeks. Businesses that relied on cloud services stayed up and running without a hitch. Those with servers on site were either down for weeks or had to move to a new location. Many companies moved to another state in order to obtain space, Internet connectivity, and electricity. Millions of companies rely on cloud services every day.

Q. I don't understand "virtual" vs. cloud.

A. Virtual systems can exist on a server in your office. For example, you can create a "virtual machine" that runs on your desktop, laptop, or server. Within that virtual machine you might have a virtual desktop computer or a virtual server. It is very common to have one physical server running two or three virtual servers.

Cloud-based servers exist outside your office, in large data centers. They consist of virtual servers running inside physical servers. But they're maintained as part of a large collection of virtual machines inside a computing center with massive bandwidth, extreme security, and very reliable power systems backed up by generators.

Cloud services are yet another layer removed from what you do in your office. Cloud services exist on very powerful computer systems that distribute the computing power across several machines – and you buy only exactly what you need. For example, your cloud-based email is inside a cluster of enterprise-level Exchange Servers. Again, they are extremely reliable, powerful, and secure.

Q. I hear about outages all the time. What do we do?

A. Actually, outages have become shorter and less frequent. They do happen, and they do disrupt business. But that's true whether your systems are in the cloud or not. The big outages that make the news generally involve the Internet backbone services such as domain name service or connectivity problems with a Tier One Internet provider. Those things disrupt everyone's business.

There was a time when people didn't want to rely on electricity for their business because it might go down. Then there was a time when people didn't want to rely on the Internet for business because it might go down. And, yes, electricity does go down. And the Internet does go down. But those occurrences are rare and short-lived. You should not base your business decisions on the exceptions to the rule. The Internet – and cloud services – are very reliable and becoming more reliable all the time.

Q. I think I can buy this a lot cheaper myself.

A. You might be able to buy some pieces cheaper by yourself. But the bundle we've put together is designed to work together to provide optimal service. You have always been able to build servers, buy firewalls, and configure everything yourself. That's not the business you're in. We have handled your technology because it is the business we're in. We have training and certifications to make sure everything is set up correctly and maintained properly. The bundle – including our services – saves you money in the long-run and makes your company more productive.

Q. If someone breaks the encryption, what can we do?

A. Given modern encryption systems, it is virtually impossible for the encryption to be broken. When you hear about break-ins to secure systems, it is never the case that someone broke through the encryption. It is always the case that they broke through a password. We can implement and enforce very strong password policies. We can also add layers called multi-factor authentication so that access requires a password and something else (e.g., finger scan or one-time-use codes).

Q. If you go away, can someone else manage our cloud services?

A. Yes. All of our services are well-known, big companies that have lots of users and resellers. If something happens to us, or you decide to move to another I.T. Service Provider, you will be able to find other professionals who can managed your cloud services. Please note that we document your entire configuration. It is extremely important that you keep a copy of this. All services are set up using your administrator@company.com account. So you can request changes, new passwords, etc. and manage everything from your existing administrator email account.

Q. Is it possible to move to a different cloud provider? What's involved?

A. Yes. Migrating to a new cloud provider is very similar to migrating from in-house to hosted services. We make a copy in the relevant cloud service (email, data storage, etc.). When everything is synchronized, we switch you over to the new cloud services. There are various ways to accomplish this, but our goal is also to minimize downtime – and that's easy to do with cloud services.

Q. Is it safe to put financial and personnel data is the cloud?

A. Yes – as long as you secure it properly. We recommend a separate storage space for sensitive data such as financial or personnel data. As a rule, only those who really need access to this information should be granted access. Password policies must be strictly enforced, since that's the weakest link. All data moves in an encrypted state, rests in an encrypted state, and is backed up in an encrypted state.

Q. Is my data safe?

A. Yes. Of course. We believe your data is safer in our cloud services than it is on a server in your office. In the cloud, everything is encrypted, backed up, and held behind world-class security systems in world-class data centers. In addition to encryption, firewalls, and digital security, the data centers have physical security. Servers are literally in locked cages behind doors with high-tech access systems, inside a secure building with guards at the doors.

Q. Is my data stored on the same server as other people's data?

A. In most cases, yes it is. But your data is completely segregated from other companies' data. You can't access each others' data. In fact, there are no systems for moving from one place in a data store to another data store. Access is only from outside the system to a specific data store. Can hacking geniuses get in? Maybe. I'm not sure how, but I'm not going to say it's impossible. I will say, it's a lot easier to break into a machine at your office.

Q. Is this like Google Apps? Is that just as good as Office?

A. The Office products we include in the bundle are the latest version of Microsoft Office. Instead of buying a CD, you are basically buying a license to use these products every month. The version we provide is installed on your machine (It's not a cloud version that can go down). So your Office suite works whether you're connected to the Internet or not. In our opinion, Microsoft Office is far superior to Google Apps. Those apps work and they provide basic functionality. If you want to be truly productive, you will get better performance from Microsoft Office – which is included in our offering at no additional charge.

Q. It doesn't make sense to pay money even when nothing goes wrong.

A. I guess this goes to the fundamental question of whether or not you believe in preventive maintenance. If you get regular safety checks, oil changes, tire rotation, and tune-ups, your car can go years without anything going wrong. Is all that effort wasted? No. One could easily argue that nothing went wrong, in large part, because you performed the maintenance.

Similarly, think about antivirus and anti-malware software. You install these and then you don't get viruses. Was that a waste of money? No. You didn't get viruses because you paid for the protection. Our bundle includes maintenance to make sure that everything is working the way it's supposed to. That has value . . . and that's why nothing goes wrong.

Q. It's too expensive.

A. No. It's not. For less than $300, you get all the core technology your company needs for up to five users. You can tear up separate bills for servers, antivirus, email security, backups, Microsoft Office, and more. Just one server with software, operating system, and maintenance will cost more than that over three years. Oh, plus the cost of electricity. And, best of all, these cloud services will be more reliable and more secure than any on-site server.

Q. Our in-house I.T. guy says we'll lose control of the data.

A. I'm not sure what that's based on. You will have ultimate control of the data. In fact, to the people who maintain the systems where your data are stored, your company name doesn't appear. Inside the cloud systems, your company information is totally anonymized. It's only inside the encrypted storage that information is visible. As long as you keep the documentation we provide – and keep it secure – you will always be able to access your data.

All services are set up using your administrator@company. com account. So you can request changes, new passwords, etc. and manage everything from your existing administrator email account. We have set it all up specifically so you cannot lose access to your data.

Q. Our Line of Business app is very old.

A. There are two options here. Some super-old services can be placed inside a virtual machine and housed at Azure or Amazon Web Services. Some cannot be virtualized for some reason. They will need to exist as physical machines on site. Obviously, we recommend that you move to an alternative, cloud-based LOB. We understand that may not be possible.

Please note that our cloud offering works perfectly in combination with physical servers and other machines. We like to have a small, "lite" server on site to provide centralized security. This may be on the same machine as the LOB, but we prefer that it be separate. Basically, we want to move as much of your business as possible to more secure, more reliable cloud services. But everything will work fine in conjunction with older systems as well.

Q. Our on-site server works fine. Why change?

A. All machines age. Older hardware is less secure. Older operating systems are less secure. Everything needs to maintained for security and performance. In the changing world of technology, things go faster and faster all the time. At some point, around three years of age, your server becomes the slowest machine in the office – simply because everything else became faster.

At some point, your server becomes the choke-point for all productivity in your office. We sold you a good, reliable, business-class server. So it will "run" for many more years. The lights will turn on. The fans will spin. But it will nevertheless become the slowest, least secure machine in the office.

You don't have to move to the cloud today. But when that server begins to hurt more than it helps, you'll need to move to something. The next, best move is to cloud services.

Q. The cloud just seems like a watered-down version of everything.

A. I'm not sure what specific experiences you've had. Today, with the right cloud offerings, you can experience the absolute best options available today. For a low monthly fee, you can access the fastest servers in the world. You can use the newest products available. You can access the fastest, safest, most reliable storage anywhere. No matter how much you spend on equipment in your office, it will be a fraction of what you can have access to for a low monthly fee.

Q. The service you recommend has only email support.

A. Some of these services have email-only support. But that is not de facto a bad thing. We have selected our partners carefully. All of them provide excellent and timely support. The fastest way for you to report a problem with us is to open a support ticket in our portal. Talking to us by phone might make you feel taken care of, but it results in a slower response than emailing us (which opens a ticket) or opening a ticket directly. How tickets are originated is a separate discussion from how good the service is.

Q. We don't have enough bandwidth.

A. This is easy to fix. Internet connections are getting faster and cheaper all the time. We have a standard process for evaluating your bandwidth, and all of your network equipment. We would be happy to perform this evaluation at no charge. We look at the bandwidth you are buying, and then take measurements at very points in your network (between the router and firewall; between the firewall and the switch; between the switch and the desktop; and over the wireless access point). Depending on the bandwidth you have and the bandwidth you might move to, we can determine which services might work better in the cloud.

Q. We like having a closed "internal" environment.

A. This is rarely true. If you have an isolated network with no Internet connectivity, then patches and updates must be applied manually and with media brought in from the outside. The requirement for USB devices or CD-ROMs to be used for moving data means that those devices are enabled company-wide . . . and are a huge potential source for viruses.

IT Professionals: This is a great example of arguing from the exception. Don't build your business model on the exceptions to the rule. Build it on the norms you actually see.

Q. We need high security for [DOD, HIPAA, SOX, etc.].

A. All of our cloud services are very secure. If you need specific documentation for compliance with HIPAA, SOX, FINRA, etc., we can provide that. Remember, all these big cloud providers make money because they are ISO 9001:2015 certified and they comply with all the various regulatory requirements. Those that provide HIPAA compliant services will sign Business Associate Agreements. All of them provide compliance information as needed.

Q. We need to spend too much money to get "cloud ready."

A. I'm not sure what you mean by this. For the most part, moving to the cloud means you will stop spending money on servers and high-end on site systems. All you really need to be cloud ready is to be willing to move to a more secure environment with better performance and less downtime.

Q. What am I investing in? I don't see the return on investment.

A. You are investing the reliability and productivity of your company. When you bought your last server, you bought a depreciating asset. We would like a server to be a good, reliable tool that lasts about three years. The IRS requires that you depreciate it over five years. So whether it's three or five, or something in between, that "investment" becomes worthless in a few years.

But that wasn't really the investment, was it? You invest in the server because it gave you centralized storage, centralized security, and delivered some business-centric services. Now, we're providing all those functions and more with cloud services. Instead of a capital expenditure that depreciates, you'll pay a monthly service fee that is an operating expense of your company. In exchange, you get access to the latest, fastest, safest computer technology available anywhere.

Q. What do we do in a disaster such as a fire?

A. Right now, if your office has a fire, you are basically out of business until we can get a new server – even a temporary one – and load your data and programs onto it. If you leave your backups at the office, you may simply be out of business.

With cloud services, a fire would simply mean that you need to go get a laptop from the office supply store and you can access all of your data and services in the cloud. They will be untouched by fires, floods, electrical outages, etc.

Q. What happens if a judge impounds a "cloud" server that has my data?

A. Judges don't generally understand technology. As cloud services have evolved, however, attorneys have hired professionals who do understand what goes on with cloud services. And unlike the stories you see on the news where prosecutors raid an office and take out all the computers, that doesn't happen with cloud services.

Judges can seize cloud "assets" – but it is done by taking over accounts, copying the data, changing passwords, and keeping people out. On rare occasions, prosecutors have worked with cloud providers to actually seize physical machines. In such cases, client data not involved in the legal action is simply hosted on a different server and keeps operating.

This is another objection that is so rare that you really shouldn't delay moving into the future based on an exception to the rule.

Q. What happens when the Internet goes down?

A. See the discussion above about outages (they're rare and becoming rarer all the time). As for what actually happens when your Internet access is down. First, your email and data are 100% safe. If you have a secondary Internet connection, that can get you back in touch with your data immediately. Email will flow into your company, and even into your phone. You can send out from your phone, and from any machine connected to a temporary hotspot.

Basically, with cloud services, you company is never "down" when the Internet is down. You just can't access it as easily. That's why we recommend a second Internet connection from a different provider. We can even set up your firewall to fail over to a cell service mi-fi device. The temporary service will probably be slower in order to keep costs down. But even slower networks are surprisingly good when all the real computing power is in the cloud.

Q. What if the data become corrupted?

A. I've never seen this in eleven years, but it's theoretically possible. We would restore from backup, which is why we maintain nightly backups of all data on a separate system. It is extremely important that you have these backups and that we provide monthly data restores from backup to verify that the backup is working.

Q. Why do we need this? We're really happy with what we have!

A. Good! We're glad you're happy. But nothing lasts forever. People were happy when they had no servers, no network, no switches, and no firewalls. But they got happier when all those things were added. At first, you may not realize all the benefits of a new technology. But eventually the benefits become clear. Just as with the move to the Internet many years ago, your move to the cloud is unavoidable. You can delay. You can put it off. But eventually you'll make the move. And then you'll look back and wonder how you ever got along without it.

Q. Why pay monthly fees for service when I can buy the software outright?

A. First, there's cash flow. The last time you bought Microsoft Office Pro Plus, you probably paid about $500. Five of those is $2,500. We've rolled that into our bundle at a fraction of the cost. Second, every time you buy software, you get a slightly different version. You might be running three different versions of Office. Standardizing everyone on the latest version will make your office more productive.

Third, there is the inevitable march of progress. Eventually, your new machines won't take your old software, or you might lose some features. Eventually, you're forced to upgrade. And a subscription may be your only option. Fourth, old software is insecure software. Software patches and fixes and only patch so much. Eventually, there are security holes that cannot be fixed. That means that old software will be vulnerable no matter how secure the rest of your network is. With our cloud bundle, you are always running the latest, safest version of the software.

Q. With encryption and de-duplication, how do I know my data won't be lost?

A. I've never seen this in eleven years, but it's theoretically possible. We would restore from backup, which is why we maintain nightly backups of all data on a separate system. It is extremely important that you have these backups and that we provide monthly data restores from backup to verify that the backup is working. So if files are deleted or even encrypted, we can restore from backup with very little downtime.

Q. You've always been our IT Pro. Are you competent in the cloud?

A. Yes – In fact we use these exact services inside our own

company. I would not ask you to buy something I didn't believe in. We believe in cloud services so much, this is what we're using for our data storage, email, antivirus, spam filtering, etc. We have gone through the training materials with all of these service providers and implemented these services both internally and with other clients.

A Few Key Take-Aways:

1. We are all moving the cloud. So start with your own company and then sell it to everyone else.

2. Start with your smallest clients. As you move to larger clients, you will have answers to all of their questions.

3. Don't memorize the practice questions and answers. But learn them so you sound very natural.

Additional Resources to Explore

- I really have nothing to point you to here, so I'll just encourage you to subscribe to my blog at blog.smallbizthoughts.com

Notes:

_____

_____

_____

_____

_____

_____

_____

_____

26. Final Thoughts: Cloud Services in a Month

When I started writing this book, I considered it a tool for accomplishing three things:

1. Educate small business IT consultants on cloud services

2. Provide a sample "business model" that you can use for the next five to ten years, based on a successful model I have used

3. Provide resources that will help you achieve success with your own cloud offering

I have to say, I was a bit surprised when this book hit 250 pages, 300 pages, and beyond. When I look at the checklists, strategies, and resource links, it turned out to be a lot more than I expected.

I sincerely hope you will digest all of this and use it to improve your business. As with *Managed Services in a Month*, I have given you what I know and what I believe. And, as with *Managed Services in a Month*, I trust that you will combine the materials in this book with your own experience and business acumen to design your own successful cloud offering.

I encourage you: Don't worry that your clients will do this all for themselves. I always hear people say, "My clients can go on Dropbox and they can do this. They can go to Intermedia and sign up for their own Exchange. So why do they need me?"

The truth is, they simply are not going to do this themselves. They've always been able to go to CDW, click a button, and get a server delivered to their office. They could have gone to Microsoft and downloaded Windows Server 2012. They didn't.

A dentist is never going to figure out that long list of services we talked about moving "one service at a time." They won't attempt to migrate everything to the cloud in an orderly fashion with zero downtime.

That's why they need you.

The Paradox of Simplicity

A few years ago, I blogged about a philosophy I have called "the paradox of simplicity." The paradox of simplicity simply amounts to this: We all think we can do everyone else's job. It looks simple. In reality, there are professionals and amateurs. And when you tackle someone else's profession, you are an amateur.

For example, I can buy Photoshop. I can resize pictures. I can even get rid of blemishes on my skin. But you would be a fool to hire me to create an advertisement for your company. There are professionals who do that. They are faster and better than me. And the result would be far superior.

The paradox of simplicity applies here as well. A client can buy a firewall, plug things in wrong, loop past the firewall, through the switch, and back out to the Internet. All the lights will turn green and they will think they have a network. In reality, they have zero protection, but it "works."

They can easily set things up wrong. But you can set it up right.

The cloud is not your enemy. The cloud is complex enough that it is absolutely your friend.

Most of the time, clients just want to do whatever they do for a living. They don't want to be in the cloud services business.

Opportunity Everywhere

I'm a huge believer that there's more opportunity in technology consulting today than at any point in our history. As all kinds of new technology take advantage of TCP/IP and other network protocols, we have the advantage.

Everyone wants to get into your business. The folks who sell office equipment have been trying to do it for twenty years. The big box stores have been trying to do it for twenty years. Even the people who install phone services have been trying to do it for more than twenty years.

Now add all the people setting up LED systems, signage, cameras, security services, key pads, license plate readers, etc., etc.

But here's the deal: It's much easier for you to learn those technologies than it is for them to learn networking!

I remember many years ago when I worked with a guy called Jimmy the Phone Guy. He was setting up a new office and called me in to help. This was in 1996. Jimmy set up the phone system and installed all the network cabling. My job was to set up a server and a dozen workstations, and to make it all work together.

This was a two-day job. One day, at lunch, Jimmy announced to me that he was going to eat my lunch. I was intrigued. Jimmy said, "One day, I'm going to take all your clients. Because, you see, I'm the phone guy. I visit every office. I make the network work. I am already a vendor in their books. All I have to learn is how to set up Windows and I'll take all your clients."

I smiled and thought, "Bring it on, Jimmy."

Well, skip ahead a bit. Twelve years later, that client called us. Her name was Debbie. She needed to save some money. Remember Debbie from Chapters Two and Three?

We talked her into ripping out that phone system and we sold her hosted PBX. We ate Jimmy's lunch. And even though I sold that company in 2011, I still get a check every month because Debbie pays her phone bill.

Your knowledge of networking will take your business into the cloud and beyond. It is your golden ticket to make money with all the amazing technology that's evolving.

You will need to continue training and learning forever. But it will pay off as you master one new technology after another. Your business might look easy to someone on the outside who doesn't understand. But your opportunities are greater than they've ever been.

So, here's your recipe for success.

Fill out those change forms. Assess your clients' networks. Start talking about The Cloud. Create your cloud offering (I recommend a Cloud Five-Pack™).

Implement your cloud solution in your business. Document absolutely everything.

Sign your first Cloud Five-Pack™ client. Send me an email when you do! karlp@smallbizthoughts.com

Move that first client to all hosted services. Document, document, document.

Sell and migrate the next client. And the next, and the next.

Fine tune your bundle and your pricing. Keep updating it every year.

Remember Kodak

As you embrace the role of cloud service provider, you need to embrace future-facing technology. Don't get stuck in the past with technology that was perfect for 2010.

Remember the history of Kodak.*

At one point, Kodak literally owned the film business. They made the film. They made the film processing chemicals and equipment. They made the paper that photos were printed on, and the machines that did the printing.

The digital camera was invented at Kodak – in 1975. But they did what too many businesses do when there's an alternative to their cash cow: They shelved it.

Kodak owns the patent on the digital camera. But they made so much money on film that there were lots of powerful people inside the company that squashed the digital products.

You probably guessed what happened. Canon, Nikon, Sony, and others paid to use that patent. They built awesome digital technology that killed Kodak's film business.

Kodak went bankrupt in 2012 and was forced to sell off their film division.

But always remember this: Someone sold the last roll of film at Kodak.

Don't be the person who installs the last server in a client's office.

In the 2020s we will experience more change than any generation in human history. So many amazing technologies are reaching critical mass at the same time that people will become overwhelmed with the speed of change.

Whether you are an "early adopter" or "late adopter," you need to be prepared for massive changes. You can either respond to whatever the world throws your way, or you can make a plan and figure out how you're going to thrive in the years ahead.

I hope this book will give you the knowledge and resources to help you be massively successful in the years ahead.

To continue the conversation online, please connect with me on social media or inside the Small Biz Thoughts Community.

As always, I thank you for your support!

– Karl P.

karlp@smallbizthoughts.com

* On Kodak's story, see:

- https://www.businessinsider.com/this-man-invented-the-digital-camera-in-1975-and-his-bosses-at-kodak-never-let-it-see-the-light-of-day-2015-8

- https://en.wikipedia.org/wiki/Steven_Sasson

- https://hbr.org/2016/07/kodaks-downfall-wasnt-about-technology

Notes:

_____

_____

_____

_____

_____

_____

_____

_____

VII. Resources: Checklists and Documentation

27. Cloud Readiness Checklist

There are two pieces to the Cloud Readiness Checklist. First, you need to look at yourself and your company. Are you ready for the cloud?

Second, you need to look at each of your clients. We did the network speed tests in Chapter Seven. But you need to know a lot more than the speed of the client's network! I recommend that you create a service ticket to complete this checklist with every client.

As for your own company, which services are you willing to provide yourself, if you have the facilities? For example, do you want clients to back up to your systems, versus a cloud service or even an on-site Server Lite? For which services are you a reseller already?

For all services that are not cloud-based, who is going to maintain them? Who's going to keep track of it? What is the monthly cost for all of these things? What kind of training do you need?

Many years ago, I considered reselling Asterisk VoIP systems. Ultimately, we decided to resell through hosted PBX. Here's why.

I was interested in going into the phone business. I built an Asterisk box and I got a SIP trunk. I installed everything, set it up, and and made it work. I configured a phone tree and added some features.

Then I thought: "If I sell this to all of my clients, I now must have somebody who knows Asterisk on staff for as long as I'm in business." With that, and I decided I didn't want to make that commitment. Instead, we committed to reselling hosted voice systems from a copy that provided everything our clients needed

– and only required us to learn sales and setup routines.

On the client side, you need to start with their bandwidth, but look at the age of their equipment, and a lot more. Old firewalls need to be replaced. Old servers probably just need to disappear.

You may end up drawing a network map for each of your clients and showing them the "before" and "after" view of their network as you plan to move them to cloud services.

As we discussed above, you need to block out what stays physical, on site, and what gets moved to virtual machines or off to cloud services.

This exercise will help you examine yourself and your clients to determine the cloud service offerings that make the most sense for you. The bad news is that you probably have to do this about once a year for the next five years. The good news is that your cloud offering will evolve as your company and clients evolve.

Basically, this checklist should prepare you for the money-making homework in Chapter Eighteen (creating cloud migration plans).

Cloud Readiness Checklist – Part One – Internal

. . . An incomplete list of items to consider as you move clients to cloud services.

1. Business Considerations

Which services can you provide in your colocation facility?

- _____

- _____

- _____

2. Which services are you a reseller or sales agent for?

- _____

- _____

- _____

3. For each process/product that exists on-site or in the cloud, answer the following questions:

Who maintains it? _____

What is the monthly Cost of the product/service? _____

What is the monthly Cost to Maintain the product? _____

What kind of training do you need for this product? (which will need to be passed on to future employees) _____

_____

What is the Probability of Downtime for this product? _

_____

- What is the source of that information? _____

What is the client's Tolerance for Downtime on this product/ service? _____

What are the Data Access / Recovery processes? _____

_____

_____

e.g., Can you get a physical copy of the data? _____

How do you recover if there's a disaster? _____

_____

_____

Is the service provider new to you or a long-term partner?

_____

4. How will you document all of this? _____

_____

_____

_____

_____

5. Number of products you need to support: _____

6. How do you make money managing and coordinating this?

_____

_____

_____

Cloud Readiness Checklist – Part Two – Client Information

1. Bandwidth Considerations

- Internet Service Provider 1 (repeat for provider 2, 3, etc.)

- Provider: _____

- Contact info / Web site: _____

- Username / Password: _____

- Additional Security information (favorite color, first school, etc.) : _____

  _____

  _____

- Line speed Up / Down: _____

- Type of connection (T-1, DSL, Cable, etc.) : _____

- Provider stats on uptime, reliability: _____

  _____

- Additional bandwidth available in this building? _____

  _____

2. Hardware Considerations

- If you have switches, firewalls, or routers that are more than three years old, they should be replaced with new, faster, smarter equipment.

- Do you need a firewall that can aggregate two Internet connections OR failover from one to another?

- If aggregating bandwidth from a single ISP, is there anything about their routing or IP address allocation that would prevent two connections from being combined successfully? _____

- What happens with the old system/equipment? For example, was it rack mounted and now you've got a big rack with a small server on it? Will equipment be "archived" in place or recycled? _____

_____

_____

_____

3. Client Procedures

You'll need to create a document for your clients on

- How to connect to email . . .

- How to connect to hosted storage . . .

- How to access the company SharePoint Server . . .

- How to connect to your remote desktop . . .

- How to connect to your LOB . . .

- How to restore files from backup . . .

- How to request assistance from your CSP (Cloud Service Provider)

- Who to call for specific functions (if not you)

NOTE: A sample of such a document is in Chapter Thirty.

4. Principle Functions: Where will each of these be located?

For each function, mark P (physical), OP (on-premises), Co (partner colocation facility), or I (Internet cloud)

Location

Function	P	OP	Co	I
• Active Directory	P	OP	Co	I
• Active Sync	P	OP	Co	I
• Blackberry	P	OP	Co	I
• Desktop Environment	P	OP	Co	I
• DHCP	P	OP	Co	I
• DNS (in-house)	P	OP	Co	I
• DNS (Internet)	P	OP	Co	I
• Domain Control	P	OP	Co	I
• Email / Exchange	P	OP	Co	I
• Firewall	P	OP	Co	I
• Internet Connection	P	OP	Co	I
• Line of Business Application	P	OP	Co	I
• Online Backup	P	OP	Co	I
• On site Backup	P	OP	Co	I
• Patch Management	P	OP	Co	I
• Printing	P	OP	Co	I

- Remote Monitoring   P OP Co I

- RWW (or Terminal Services)   P OP Co I

- Sharepoint   P OP Co I

- Spam Filter   P OP Co I

- SQL   P OP Co I

- Storage/File Store   P OP Co I

- Telephone   P OP Co I

- Terminal Server   P OP Co I

- Virus Protection (&Spyware)   P OP Co I

- VPN (hardware)   P OP Co I

- VPN (via Server RRAS)   P OP Co I

- WWW   P OP Co I

- Other: P OP Co I

- Other: P OP Co I

- Other: P OP Co I

5. SBS Components Enabled

- AD / Logon services

- DHCP

- DNS (in-house)

- Domain Control (FSMO Roles)

- Exchange

- On site Backup

- Printing

- RWW

- SharePoint

- SQL (SBS Premium)

- Storage/File Store

- Terminal Server (SBS Premium)

- VPN (via Server RRAS)

- WWW

6. Cloud Service Provider Info to Track (repeat for each provider)

- Administrative web site (for product purchase, accounting, etc.) _____

- Tool management web site (to add users, configure services, etc.) _____

- Tech Support web site and information needed to get support: _____

- Tech Support phone number, email, or other contact info: _____

Resources Mentioned

- **Asterisk PBX** – asterisk.org/get-started/applications/what-is-an-ip-pbx

Notes:

_____

_____

_____

_____

_____

_____

_____

_____

28. Robocopy Samples

In Chapter Fifteen we walked through the Robocopy commands we recommend for migrating data to the cloud and for creating a backup job to bring it back down after the cloud has become your primary data store.

Here we present those Robocopy jobs again, as you might enter them into a script. These scripts are included in your downloads as .txt files. As presented, they are not executable.

To create executable scripts from these, edit in Notepad or your favorite text editor and save as .bat (batch) files.

For testing purposes, I always put a Pause command at the end. That way, I can just double-click the .bat file, it will run, and then it will stay on the screen for me to see. Without a Pause, it just finishes and closes the CMD window.

Luckily, you can send a Robocopy job to a .log file and capture pretty much everything you need. But sometimes, the command window gives you more information (and faster). For example, if there's a permission error, the .log file won't be created.

So, tweak your Robocopy jobs until it looks like they're doing everything you need to do. Then schedule them with Task Scheduler. See Chapter Fifteen for more details.

R1: Robocopy to Cloud Storage Checklist

Overview

Background: You have signed up for Jungle Disk (or another cloud storage provider) and installed the workgroup agent on the server. Now we will move a "backup" of the core data store into the cloud. After this synchronization is complete, you will go through the process of making the cloud storage into the live data store.

1. Complete a Cloud Migration Plan

- See Cloud Migration Plan document from Chapter Eighteen

2. Document the Robocopy setup and credentials

- See Hosted Services Inventory document from Chapter Thirty-Two

3. Verify the exact data to be copied to cloud storage:

Local Asset Location	Cloud Location
e.g., E:\LocalDataBlob*.*	R:\CompanyData
_____	_____
_____	_____
_____	_____

4. Write the script to move data from Local Storage Area to Cloud

See sample script in text file "Robo Transition E to R.txt"

```
rem last updated karlp 20190610
rem date stamp
c:
cd \!Tech
del ~robo_e2r.bak
rename ~robo_e2r.log ~robo_e2r.bak


echo /\/\/\/\/\/\/ >> C:\!Tech\~robo_e2r.log
echo \/\/\/\/\/\/\ >> C:\!Tech\~robo_e2r.log
date /t >> C:\!Tech\~robo_e2r.log
time /t >> C:\!Tech\~robo_e2r.log


robocopy „E:\LocalDataBlob" R:\ /xd "E:\
LocalDataBlob\Finance\bwdata" /e /r:1 /w:1 /
mt:12 /rh:2000-0459 /log:c:\!Tech\~robo_e2r.log


robocopy „E:\LocalDataBlob\Finance\bwdata" M:\
/e /r:1 /w:1 /mt:12 /log:c:\!Tech\~robo_e2o.log


Pause
```

5. Test the batch job

a. Connect to the Server
b. Browse to the C:\!Tech directory
c. Find and execute (double click on) the batch file above, e.g., Robo_e2r.bat
d. Verify that the file runs and that files are being copied. If you need to stop the batch file, simple press CTRL-C
e. You should be able to open and read the .log file in C:\!Tech\~robo_e2r.log

6. Schedule the batch job to run in a small window of time (e.g., 8 PM to 1 AM)

    a.   Connect to the Server

    b.   Run Task Scheduler

    c.   In the right-hand window click on the "Create Task …" option

    d.   Fill out the details to run the batch job you just created

    e.   When you go to save, enter the username that will be used for executing the job

        • Make sure this is a user that is an administrator or backup operator created just for jobs like this

Note: You only have to select a start time in the Task Scheduler since the run hours are set in the batch job.

. . . the next day . . .

7. Verify that the job ran without errors

    a.   Open and review the log file you created (e.g., C:\!Tech\~robo_e2r.log)

    b.   Look in the cloud drive location to verify that files were copied there (e.g., R:\)

8. Adjust, fine tune, monitor

    a.   Let the job run every night. Adjust the run window until it settles down and stops using resources (disc, memory, network) at least an hour before the client shows up for work.

    b.   Run continuously every night until you make the cloud storage system "live"

R2: Robocopy Backup from Cloud Storage

Overview

Background: You have finished copying all server data to the cloud. In this example, you have two storage areas, mapped as "R" for most data, and "M" for financial data (M is for money).

You have made the cloud storage live. In other words, it is the primary data store and now it needs to be backed up.

This script backs up the cloud storage every night by bringing a copy down to the local machine in new "backup" folders.

See sample script in text file "Robo Back from Cloud.txt"

```
rem last updated karlp 20190701
rem date stamp
c:
cd \!Tech
del ~BackFromCloud1.bak
del ~BackFromCloud2.bak
rename ~BackFromCloud1.log ~BackFromCloud1.bak
rename ~BackFromCloud2.log ~BackFromCloud2.bak


echo /\/\/\/\ >> C:\!Tech\~BackFromCloud1.log
echo \/\/\/\/ >> C:\!Tech\~BackFromCloud1.log
date /t >> C:\!Tech\~BackFromCloud1.log
time /t >> C:\!Tech\~BackFromCloud1.log


robocopy R:\ E:\Backup\CompanyData /e /r:3 /w:3
/mt:12 /log:c:\!Tech\~BckFromCloud1.log


echo /\/\/\ >> C:\!Tech\~BackFromCloud2.log
echo \/\/\/ >> C:\!Tech\~BackFromCloud2.log
date /t >> C:\!Tech\~BackFromCloud2.log
time /t >> C:\!Tech\~BackFromCloud2.log
```

```
robocopy M:\ E:\Backup\SensitiveData /e /r:3
/w:3 /mt:12 /log:c:\!Tech\~BackFromCloud2.log


echo /\/\/\ >> C:\!Tech\~BackFromCloud2.log
echo \/\/\/ >> C:\!Tech\~BackFromCloud2.log
date /t >> C:\!Tech\~BackFromCloud2.log
time /t >> C:\!Tech\~BackFromCloud2.log


Pause
```

Schedule this and then repeat steps 6, 7, and 8 from above.

Notes:

_____

_____

_____

_____

_____

_____

_____

_____

29. Client Onboarding Checklist

Onboarding Checklist for Cloud Five-Pack™

The checklist below is for setting up new clients on Managed Services and Cloud Services. It is designed for somewhat larger companies but works fine with smaller companies as well. By larger companies I simply mean those that actually have departments.

The checklist starts in the "administrative" department or front office. Somebody determines what the overall contract covers, enters setup fees, and then sets up the client information in QuickBooks, the PSA, the ticketing systems, and so forth.

After that, you will use a column to signify which work is done by administrative staff, technical staff, and customer service staff. The checklist is routed back and forth so that you can make sure nothing is missed.

The beautiful thing about checklists is that they allow you to have replicable success and make sure that you don't miss any steps. You lose money by having inconsistencies. Every time someone says, "Oh man, we totally forgot to set up the automatic payments" (or whatever), your company just lost some money.

In the example here, the salesperson is going to create a service ticket with a time estimate of about one-and-a-half hours. Everyone who is involved is going to use the PSA to keep track of the checklist.

Every time you move a client to cloud services, you will have better and better estimates of how long it actually takes you in the administrative part, in the technical part, and so forth. Always update the checklist. It will get better over time.

Now, let's walk through it very quickly.

- Check to see that the names match between the PSA, QuickBooks, your mailing list, etc.

- Create an invoice for the setup and monthly fees.

- Calculate the fees. If payment is by credit card, set up the recurring payments.

  In my companies, we asked companies to prepay for everything on the first of the month. If they pay by credit card, it is charged on the first of the month. If people don't want to do that, and they want to pay with a check, we require them to pay three months in advance.

  We don't require this to be on a calendar quarter. I'm happy to have them on any three months in a row that they want. That way, the money doesn't come in in large bumps.

  As it turns out, from our experience, the companies who insist on paying by check tend to be larger companies because they don't have a process for putting that much money onto a credit card. That's fine with me. So our largest clients send us these really big checks because they're paying three months in advance.

  We insist on being prepaid so we will never have collections. We spend no time collecting money. We have no accounts receivable. That has never done us any harm ever in the history of our company. As a result, we don't have any losses or write-offs.

- An administrative assistant (not a technician) calls the client and gets a list of contacts in case there's an emergency after hours. We enter that information in the PSA.

- If this is an existing client, you need to finish up old contracts. Verify that billing is correct. Cancel those contracts in the

PSA and create a new one.

- The admin then changes the ticket status to "schedule this" or "ready to work" or whatever your status is that allows a technician to pick it up. At that point, the checklist moves to the Tech Support department.

  You may be using physical, paper checklists for this. I actually prefer that's as electronic checklists are sometimes lost or forgotten. Either way, you may want to have a system for tracking how many onboarding checklists you have in circulation. If you're going to move 10 or 20 clients onto cloud services all at once, you want to keep a master list of how many of these are in progress.

- Now the checklist is in the tech department. Now we address tasks that *do* require some technical skills. This includes updating the managed services grid, which is the list of all of the machines and all of the services that you've deployed. We keep that in an Excel spreadsheet so we can side-check what's being charged to us and what we are charging people in the PSA.

- Deployment begins! Install the remote monitoring agent on the server and then run whatever process you have to detect the other devices and install the RMM agent on all of those.

- Add servers to the daily monitor and patch management list.

- Set up maintenance jobs and make sure you document everything. For example, when we create a new backup process, we write out a narrative (just a paragraph or two) that describes the backup.

- Update the daily monitoring sheets to make sure that all devices are on it.

- We create a client-specific monthly maintenance checklist. Remember: Managed services means there are certain things you do every month at part of the maintenance of the operating systems, software, and network. In the days of automated patch management and remote monitoring, most of that is done by services that run all the time. It used to be that we would go on site and check how much free disk space they had once a month. Now it's done every 60 seconds. So, we don't have to put every little check on our Monthly Maintenance checklist. We just need to make sure that those checks are in place and that they're not being ignored.

- Once everything is working, we update the ticket to show that we've completed all these steps. Then the checklist is routed to the customer service department.

- Someone in the customer service department must train the clients' users. Note that this is something that does not require a technician, in my opinion. You don't need an MCSE to train a client on how to open a ticket in the portal.

- And, of course, the customer service department sends the client a welcome letter.

- The checklist now returns to the tech department.

- Technicians then setup the web email, storage, antivirus, and so forth.

- And finally, at the end, the customer service department trains users on email, spam filtering, email encryption, and whatever else you've sold them.

Obviously, you will have much more detailed checklists for each of the processes within the technical setup. There should be distinct documentation for setting up email accounts, setting up the BDR, and so forth.

-- -- --

Client Onboarding Checklist - Managed Services and Cloud Services

New Client / Signer: _____

Date: _____

Signed Deal (circle one)   Silver - Gold - Platinum

First Month on Service will be:

Jan Feb Mar Apr May Jun Jul Aug Sep Oct Nov Dec

Cover Sheet

\# of Servers: _____

Cost for Servers: _____

\# of Workstations: _____

Cost for Workstations: _____

Cloud Five-Pack™s   _____

Cost for Cloud Five-Pack™s _____

Cloud Five-Pack™ MS _____

Cloud Five-Pack™ MS _____

Other   _____

Cost Other   _____

Other   _____

Cost Other   _____

Total Monthly: _____

Setup Fees: _____

Setup to be paid by (circle one)   Check   Credit Card

Monthly to be paid by   Check   Credit Card

                               (3 months)   each month

Correct Billing Information:

Company _____

Name   _____

Address 1 _____

Address 2 _____

City / State / Zip _____

Contact Phone _____

Party Responsible	Date Completed

Admin Dept.

1. Account Setup / Update

2. Create Service Request (time estimate 1.5 hrs)

3. Check to see that the names match how they want to be billed for services:

- PSA
- QuickBooks
- Mailing List

4. Create Invoices for Setup / monthly

5. Calculate first month fees + setup   **Sales Dept.**

6. Collect Money   **Admin Dept.**

- If Credit Card:
  - Collect Credit Card form
  - Charge Credit card: initial setup fees/first month
  - Apply payments in QB
  - Set up Autopay & Monthly recurring
  - Remove old recurring charges from credit card

- If Check:

  - Collect check from client (3 months + setup) Sales
  - Apply payments in QB   Admin
  - Hand off check for depositing . . . to . . .

7. Identify three people to be listed in our call down list in the event of a server down

8. File all paperwork generated to this point

9. If existing client, create credits as needed for Email Filtering, monitoring, other services

10. Expire old service agreements in PSA

11. Create new service agreements in PSA

- Set the new service agreements in PSA to be the default agreement

12. Change Ticket to "Schedule This"

Tech Dept:

1. Setup Monitoring and Patch Management

2. Update Managed Services Grid

3. Install RMM agent on server (create Ticket)

4. In RMM, set network detect to inventory all attached devices. Determine which of these need agents and deploy agents.

5. Add server to RMM daily monitoring and verify

6. Add server to RMM patch management and verify

7. Set up back up jobs and document narrative

8. Update daily monitoring sheet to include new client requirements

9. If new client, create the Monthly Maintenance checklist

10. If existing client, check existing Monthly Maintenance checklist for compliance.

11. Verify that RMM Agent and AV are working on all devices

12. Update Ticket to show we have completed these steps

Customer Service Dept:

1. Train Client on . . .

- PSA portal
- Ticketing process

2. Send intro letter to client

Tech Department

Setup Web, Email, Other Services

1. (If client requires Web Site)

- Take control of DNS or communicate with whoever manages it
- Set up Hosting Service
- Copy files if flat web site or set up WordPress and forward credentials
- Document all aspects of web hosting service

2. Storage

- Set up Jungle Disk per separate checklist
- This client requires the following storage spaces:
  o Company-Wide Folders
  o Admin/Financial/Personnel Folders
  o Other _____

- Storage setup will be:

  o Primary Storage in Cloud / Backed up to _____
  _____

  o Primary Storage Local / Backed up to Cloud
  o Other (describe): _____
  _____

3. Email and Office

- Email and Office apps provided through: _____
  _____

  (e.g., Sherweb / Intermedia / Rackspace / Appriver)

- Obtain list of all users and emails required for each

  (Note: Get this in written format and copy/paste. Do not re-type this information.)

- Create email accounts per separate checklist
- Set up Email Filtering, if appropriate
- Migrate email per separate checklist
- For each user, determine whether Office Apps are needed. Document apps needed per user
- Include:
  o MS Office Pro
  o MS Office Pro Plus (Access)
  o Skype
  o Email Archiving
  o Email OWA
  o Email Encryption
- Allocate Office licenses per user
- Install Office licenses per user
- If client is using Sharepoint, create a project for this

Customer Service Dept:

1. Train Client on . . .

- Email (Spam) Filtering
- Office License username/pw
- Email Archiving
- OWA
- Email Encryption

Note: Everyone who touches this form (administrative staff, technicians, and customer services) must update this checklist if there are any changes.

Last Action:

When all complete, put this form in filing in-box

30. New User Welcome Package

In Chapter Twenty-Seven I mentioned creating a new employee welcome document. In addition to helping your clients improve their own employee onboarding process, this document can make you more valuable as a business partner.

Here's the setup:

I know you've had a client call you at nine o'clock on Monday morning and say, "We have a new employee starting today. I need you to set up a machine."

This is frustrating because you know that they went through a process something like this:

- Decide we need a new person
- Define the job
- Created an ad
- Advertise the position
- Collect résumés
- Interview people
- Make an offer
- Hire someone. Agree on first day of work.

In other words, they've been working on this for a long time and only engaged you at the last minute.

With this form, you can insert yourself in their process and create a bullet point that says

- Create a Service Ticket with new username, email address, workstation, and required software/services

If they create a service ticket, your team can perform all of the new-user setup remotely. And it's not an urgent, last minute request. Depending on your PSA, ticketing system, or web site, you could even gather all the necessary details in a form within the ticket.

With a ticket in place, you can set up the new employee with a logon into the Windows system, access to QuickBooks if needed, and all the other services they need.

The document below simply informs the new employee of how they access each of these services, what their username is for each service, and so forth. You provide this document in PDF format to your primary contact. They hand it off to their new employee as part of their onboarding process.

With a process such as this, you move beyond doing technical work – you are truly helping them have a more efficient business. You are now helping your clients improve their internal processes. With luck, they will see the value of having you as their partner and see that you're not just the company that fixes the computers.

Note that you must customize this document for each client and get them to enter that service ticket before the next new employee shows up.

Of course this is all billable as and Add/Move/Change.

Note that I use my company as an example. So search for references to SBT, GLB, Small Biz Thoughts, and Great Little Book and replace as needed.

-- -- --

New Employee Orientation

A Quick Intro to the Tools We Use

This document gives a brief introduction to the most important information and tools you'll use at SBT/GLB (Small Biz Thoughts / Great Little Book).

You'll find that we place a premium on consistency, reproducibility, and documentation. If you find that our processes have evolved beyond what is described in this document, please bring it to your supervisor's attention so we can update this document.

Some tools are only used by specific people (e.g., QuickBooks and Salesforce.com). If a section does not apply to you, it has been crossed off. If a section is blank but has not been crossed off, contact your supervisor for logon information, etc.

Logon

We use a Windows-based computer system. Your username is not case sensitive but your password is.

Your Username is: _____

Your Pass Phrase is: _____

The domain name is GLB (or GLB.local in some cases)

Always use your own logon to access systems at GLB. Do not share your password except with a technician in the performance of troubleshooting.

As a general rule, our technical support team will change your password if they need to log on as you for any reason. When this happens, they will leave you a note with your new password. Please change it as soon as you can.

Access the QuickBooks Server Remotely

If you have been given remote access rights, you can connect to our QuickBooks Server from the outside world. Here's how:

1. Run "Remote Desktop Connection"

2. Enter the server address gaga.remote:9995

3. Enter your Windows domain user ID and password from the section above. If you are asked to accept a certificate, do so.

4. Once you see the server desktop, click on the QuickBooks icon to open the program.

Your QuickBooks Username is: _____

Your QuickBooks Pass Phrase is: _____

Exchange Email

Our email is a hosted Exchange Email account. Your desktop computer has been set up to access this.

Your Email Address is: _____

Your Email Pass Phrase is: _____

Online CRM (Customer Relationship Management)

Open a browser and go to www.smbbooks.com/admin

Your Username is: _____

Your Pass Phrase is: _____

PayPal Merchant Services

We use PayPal Merchant Services. You access via www.paypal.com.

Your PayPal Username is: _____

Your PayPal Pass Phrase is: _____

Password "Vault"

We use the program TK8 Safe to store passwords for all accounts. This program is very secure and all passwords are encrypted.

Do not store SBT/GLB related passwords in Word, Excel, text files, or any other program.

Do not write down passwords on paper.

Major passwords (banks, online store, PayPal, etc.) are changed about once per month. If you try to log in and cannot, please ask for the new password.

As a general rule, our internal email is considered secure. If you need to exchange passwords, do so by internal encrypted email. Do not send passwords through external email systems such as Gmail or Hotmail.

Where We Keep Stuff

Other than QuickBooks, all company files are kept on the "S" drive in the cloud. Here are some notes on organization.

First, we have a few "permanent" folders off the S:\ root. But almost everything you'll work with is in a year-based folder, such as S:\GLB2015 or S:\GLB2016. So, for example, all Marketing for 2016 will be in the S:\GLB2016\Marketing folder.

If you need something for the new year (e.g., 2020) and it is not where you think it should be, you can copy (not move) it from the previous year. You may need to recreate the entire folder structure to make this work.

File names should start with the most important word you'll be looking for. So, if you want to find a procedure related to calculating payroll, it will be named "Payroll Calculation." That way, you can find things quickly because the file will begin with the word you're looking for.

There are no personal folders. All company files are related to company departments or tasks. Marketing goes in Marketing, Operations goes in Operations, etc.

Date formats should be consistent. It is often helpful to include a date within a file name. For example, "Karl Slide Deck 20191110. pptx".

Our official company date format is YYYYMMDD, or YYYY MM DD. Do not use any other date formats within file names.

Procedures are in the \Operations\Procedures folder. Sometimes there are subfolders. All files here should strictly follow the naming conventions.

All procedures should be updated every time you use them. This will make them better and better.

Note: You must change every password on this document, enter the new passwords into your password vault, and DO NOT write down the new passwords.

Our Official Address
Our official address for 99% of all transactions is:
12345 6th Street, #789
Springfield, USA 95819

Our company telephone number is (916) 555-1212

Your extension is _____

Notes:

31. Monthly Maintenance Checklist

No matter where you are in the evolution of your cloud service offering, you need to do regular monthly maintenance. After all, maintenance is the core of any managed service business. So this document looks at the monthly tasks you need to perform for your clients.

No matter what's in the cloud, you'll be in a hybrid environment with some equipment on site for several years.

Monthly Maintenance Checklist for Managed Service Clients

Checklist updated: November 20, 2019

Date: _____

Client:

Client Name _____

Client address line 1 _____

Client address line 2 _____

City / State / Zip _____

Technician: _____

Monthly Performed Remote?   Y / N

Contact:

Contact name _____

Contact phone number _____

Check each box only after it is done. If an item cannot be done, circle it and write a note to explain. If an item does not apply put an X in the box and write a note to explain.

If an item needs to be updated, deleted, etc. put edit notes in the left page border and an arrow to the item.

1) Client Check-In and Monthly Single

- ☐ When performing the Monthly Maintenance on site, check with the client contact for any new or outstanding issues and enter them in the "Issues" section of this checklist. (Last page)
- ☐ Check the ticketing system for all outstanding Service Requests (not assigned to Back Office).
- ☐ Print out a prioritized list if necessary.
- ☐ Print out the Monthly Single for this month and attach it to this monthly maintenance checklist. (A Monthly Single is a single maintenance item that only needs to be executed once or twice a year. We pick one such task each month and perform it across all clients.)
- ☐ Complete all steps detailed in the Monthly Single before continuing on unless specifically noted otherwise in the Monthly Single.

2) System Backup

☐ Check the Backup Job Monitor and Alerts sections, evaluate and clean up as needed. Do not leave more than one month of data unless there is an ongoing issue.

☐ Record the number of good backups in the last 30 days: _ _____ Note: 20 successful is ideal.

☐ Identify the most recent (discs)(tapes) in rotation that are indicated to contain a successful backup.

☐ Verify that each full server OS backup contained in the target backup set has the complete System State for that server.

☐ Verify backup of critical OS files, Data files, and Exchange Mailboxes by restoring the following items:
   o %System root%\repair directory
   o C:\Program Files\Veritas\backup Exec\NT\ Catalogs directory
   o A sample of files from the client's data directory

Note: All data is redirected to temp\Backup Test

   o Select mailbox items from any active user

Note: All email is redirected to Administrator

☐ Log into the Administrator email account and verify the emails targeted for restore were in fact restored.

☐ Clean up the Administrators inbox by moving important company info to the "Keep This" folder in the Inbox and deleting all useless items.

☐ Remove any data restored to the temp\Backup Test folder.

☐ Move the media going off site for the End-of-Month Backup to the Retired Media set.

☐ If performing the Monthly remotely, perform an Eject Tape/Disc function now.

☐ Verify that the End-of-Month (Discs)(Tapes) have been write protected.

☐ Verify that the End-of-Month (Discs)(Tapes) have each

been properly labeled.

☐ Record the (Discs)(Tapes) going off site here: _____
_____

☐ Record the number of ((Discs)(Tapes) Model) Backup Tapes available: _____

If there are less than 6 (Discs)(Tapes) available (12 for a two-media scheme, etc.) create a ticket to deliver and label new tapes or discs.

☐ Verify the tape drive has been cleaned – Three times for a DAT and once for DLT or SLR._

☐ When performing the Monthly Maintenance remotely, have the on site contact perform the operation and verify they have marked the tape for the number of uses._

☐ Cleaning cartridge needed Yes / No

☐ If a Cleaning Cartridge is needed, either create a ticket to deliver a new Cleaning Cartridge or add it to an existing Tape ticket._

☐ If there is a ticket to deliver and label discs or a box of tapes, or a cleaning cartridge, perform the work necessary to complete that ticket now._

Note: Be certain to enter the product into the ticket immediately.

☐ Verify the Backup Log has been updated with notes on:_
  o Tape cleaning
  o Restore verification
  o End-of-Month (discs)(tapes) going off site

☐ Update the Network Documentation Binder Tech Notes with other relevant information from this section._

☐ Note all unresolved problems from this section in the "Issues" section._

☐ When performing the Monthly Maintenance remotely, verify the on site contact has made any appropriate entries for this section in the NDB._

3)   Other Network, Company, and User Specific Items

☐ Bandwidth Test www.speakeasy.net/speedtest

1st: Download _____ kb/s   Upload _____ kb/s

2nd: Download _____ kb/s   Upload _____ kb/s

☐ Update the Network Documentation Binder Tech Notes with relevant information from this section._
☐ Note all unresolved problems from this section in the "Issues" section._
☐ When performing the Monthly Maintenance remotely, verify the on-site contact has made any appropriate entries for this section in the NDB._

4)   Issues - New and Outstanding (Client Contact, Update section, Users, etc.)

_____

_____

_____

_____

_____

5)   Client Check Out

☐ Verify that the previously verified tapes have been delivered to the client contact to be placed offsite
☐ Check with Client Contact and convey status on all outstanding issues (in person, on phone, or by email)_
☐ Discuss any recommendations based on this monthly maintenance with the Client Contact as needed

☐ Draft the Monthly Maintenance Follow Up email using the appropriate KPE template

Note: You must CC the Service Manager and Monitor

☐ When performing the Monthly Maintenance on site, make a final round check with all users, especially those who had issues to be resolved

6)   Service Requests and Products

☐ If required, create Service Requests for all unresolved issues._

☐ Update the client's Monthly Maintenance Service request with all of the following:
   o   Travel Time
   o   Mileage
   o   Expenses (if possible)
   o   Time on task
   o   Detailed work documentation including Internal Analysis notes
   o   Product delivered to the client. Billable or Not (Tapes, cleaning cartridges, cables, etc.)

Monthly Maintenance Complete _____

7)   Monthly Maintenance Checklist Update

☐ Update the client's Monthly Maintenance Checklist document with all necessary revisions._

Notes:

_____

_____

_____

_____

_____

_____

_____

_____

32. Cloud Documentation Sample

One of the things that has to happen from now on is that you have to document some stuff that we haven't traditionally documented. You have to be able to give the client something that says, "Your data are stored *here* and this is how you access it."

Think about what could happen if you don't document this. Let's say the client gets a new manager and your company is replaced. Without documentation, your client literally has no idea where their data are.

We are entering an era where critically important data is stored in cloud services without documentation. Companies will lose their data forever. It will be up in some cloud, somewhere. Maybe even backed up for the rest of eternity, but no one can ever access it.

That kind of thing will happen if you don't document these services properly.

We already have clients who lose their own domain names because they didn't renew it and they thought you were going to renew it, and you're not responsible because their last IT guy has the domain name but they don't even remember what his name is. That's the tip of the iceberg of what people can lose if they don't keep their cloud services documented properly.

Even if you use a documentation tool such as IT Glue, I'm a big fan of having your documentation in a physical binder, and of giving the client a copy in PDF format.

The client paid for the network. They paid for the services. They paid for your time. It's their information. It's their documentation. And I think they should have a copy.

However you document it, please document it!

Quick Inventory

Hosted Services

Date: _____

Client / Prospect: _____

Technician: _____

Client Contact: _____

Client Email: _____

Client Location: _____

_____

_____

ISP for this location: _____

IP Address Range [DHCP] [Static] _____

_____

Internet Domain Name: _____

Domain Registrar: _____

Domain Registry Contact: _____

Domain Technical Contact: _____

Domain Billing Contact: _____

Domain Name Server 1: _____

Domain Name Server 2: _____

Domain Name Server 3: _____

Domain Name Records:

Host	Record Type	Address / Info

Web Site Hosted at: _____

Web Site Managed by: _____

Web Site Type (e.g., WordPress, DreamWeaver, Blogger) _____

_____

Email Hosted at: _____

Email Managed by: _____

Email Information: _____

Spam Filtering Hosted at: _____

Spam Filtering Managed by: _____

Hosted Storage at: _____

Hosted Storage Managed by: _____

Hosted Storage Information: _____

Description of Backup: _____

_____

_____

_____

_____

Where is primary company data stored? _____

_____

Who manages this? _____

Describe the Antivirus Solution: _____

_____

_____

_____

_____

Describe the company's firewall and network security: _

_____

_____

_____

_____

_____

Other Notes:

_____

_____

_____

_____

_____

33. Removing Clients from Cloud Services

Hey, stuff happens, right? At some point, you might lose a client.

This checklist is designed as a way to create an orderly process for removing clients from your services. But, at the same time, it is designed to make it easy for clients to continue to use some of your services.

I have built two IT companies, bought one and folded it into my operations, and sold off all of them. BUT, I still manage the domain name registration, DNS, and web hosting for almost every client we've ever had. Plus, we still get paid for phone services we sold way back when.

In other words, I have recurring revenue from people who haven't been managed service clients for years.

I put this checklist together in response to a question I got. I have never removed a client from cloud services, so I had to speculate about how I'd do that. This checklist is included in the downloads for this book.

Now, let's walk through the checklist.

First, who is the client and on what date will the service be terminated?

Who at the client's office is our primary contact during the transition?

Is the client going to be moving services to another provider? If so, you need to know that company.

And here's the key to success: You ask your clients, "**Which services do you want to keep with us** – domain name registration, hosted email, website, telephone, spam, antivirus, BDR, patch management?"

I will let a client keep all these services. Theoretically, if somebody wanted to leave me, I'd keep all those services and have no labor involved. I would absolutely sell that every day and every night. And then, if they need labor, I'll tell them to talk to an IT service provider I know.

Once you know what they're keeping and what's going, you need to prepare a "what's next" memo. This memo is based on what we use when someone leaves our standard managed services. First, all labor is billable from now on. Once a client gives us written notice, nothing is free and nothing is in arrears.

We require the client to buy a block of labor (hours). We work tickets against that block of time. When everything is disconnected and we're all settled, we give the client a refund of whatever money we did not use. I promise.

Our memo also informs them that machines may be left in an unsafe state. If the client is willing to pay us for antivirus, for example, then they'll be safe. But if we uninstall our antivirus and they don't want to pay for another, we need to inform them of the danger. The same is true for Windows updates, security patches, and remote monitoring.

We'll be happy to set things up for a client who is leaving – we're not irresponsible – but we will charge for it. So, when a client leaves us, that's an add/move/change, and that's billable.

All of this is spelled out in our contract on day one.

We also remind them that the contract forbids them from hiring our employees without compensating us. And that clause holds for twelve months after the contract is over.

And, of course, some contracts such as the BDR have to stay in place. Even if they're not paying us, they have to pay whatever their bill is.

Next, we route the "departure ticket" to our admin department. They review the account. If there are any accounts receivable, arrangements need to be made for payment. The admin will also make sure that we get the prepayment for the block of hours and set the expiration date for the managed service agreement.

If necessary, they will change the client's terms in QuickBooks.

We ask whether the client would still like to receive our newsletter. You never know: You might lure them back one day.

Next, the ticket is routed to the tech department. They create a billable service ticket to remove the client from managed services.

If removing from domain name management, create a billable ticket to do that. Domains are important and you need to make sure you do the right thing here. If someone loses their domain because of your sloppiness, that could be very expensive.

You need to make sure you do whatever it takes so that the client knows where their domain name is registered, when it expires, and who can access the registration info. If it's not you it's got to be somebody else.

One of the reasons I have hundreds of domains under my management is that clients don't know how to deal with this. And every time it comes up, I get an email and I send them an invoice. I charge a premium for domain name registration (probably three to five times the norm). Clients could shop around. But nobody ever does.

Removing the client from website hosting is the same. It's billable. Document it. Who's responsible? If something breaks, here's who you can call.

The same holds for hosted exchange or hosted email, and all other services.

This document is designed so that, when you put this in front of a client, they see that cloud services are complicated. They see how involved it is, how much you need to keep track of, etc. And then they see that all of that was only costing them (for example) $250 a month!

So, the bottom line is that you have to document everything and perform an orderly hand-off. It might be a hand-off to the client or to another IT service provider.

As I said before, you need to do this the right way. Be the good guys. Act with integrity. You never know what the future holds.

Finally, when all your stuff is uninstalled, transitioned to something else, and you're done, done, done, then you can close the service ticket and disable their account.

Of course, the last thing on the checklist is to update the checklist.

-- -- --

Checklist – Remove Client from Cloud and Managed Services

Client: _____

Date service will stop: _____

Who at client office is our primary contact during transition?

_____

Contact Phone _____

Contact Email _____

Will client be moving to services from another provider?

Yes   No

If yes, company:_____

Contact Phone: _____

Contact Email: _____

Which services will client **keep with us?**

- ☐ Domain Name Registration
- ☐ Web Site Hosting
- ☐ Hosted Email
- ☐ Telephone Service
- ☐ Spam Filtering
- ☐ Antivirus
- ☐ Hosted Storage
- ☐ BDR
- ☐ Remote Monitoring
- ☐ Patch Management
- ☐ Microsoft Office
- ☐ (including _____ Email Archiving, _____ Email Encryption)
- ☐ Other: _____
- ☐ Other: _____
- ☐ Other: _____

Step One: Client Communications

Send the "What's Next" Memo to client:

> *Note that all labor to remove the client from managed services is billable (as an add/move/change it would not be covered under managed service).*

Note that the machines may be left in an unsafe state. Unless there's a billable ticket to turn on updates of some type, the machines will not receive critical updates after you remove your RMM (remote monitoring and management) agent. If antivirus is included in your service, the machines will be without antivirus unless there's a billable ticket to install something.

Please remember that your contract forbids you from hiring our employees without compensating us.

Note that your company has and will abide by a non-disclosure agreement with regard to all of your data and network configurations.

We will assist your new tech support (internal or external) with the transition. All labor related to the transition will be billable.

We will provide you with all documentation and a summary of all outstanding issues with your systems (if any).

Clarify with the client that other contracts will remain in place (e.g., BDR, HAAS, or telephone).

Step Two – Route to Admin Dept.

- ☐ Review client's account
- ☐ If there are any accounts receivable, make arrangements for payment.
- ☐ Contact client to inform them that all work to remove them from service is billable and all labor must be paid in advance.
- ☐ Collect prepayment of $_____ for _____ hours labor.
- ☐ Cancel automated recurring billing at merchant service.
- ☐ Set expiration date for Managed Service Monthly Recurring billing contracts in PSA.

☐ Leave Billable Time and Materials contract in place and active.

☐ Leave other monthly contracts in place (BDR, telephones, etc.).

☐ If client will continue with "un-bundled" services, create recurring billing for these.

☐ If necessary, change client "terms" in QuickBooks.

☐ Will client still receive our newsletter? (Yes)(No)

☐ If no, remove them from the newsletter mailing list.

Step Three – Route to Tech Dept.

☐ Create a billable service ticket to remove client from managed service. This is a catch-all for items not listed in the ticket below.

☐ Note: All work related to removing agents, services, etc. from managed services is billable and should be logged against this ticket.

If removing Domain Name Registration management:

☐ Create a billable ticket to remove Domain Name Registration management

☐ Determine where domain will be housed and who will be responsible

☐ Execute the domain transfer process

☐ Verify domain has new information in WHOIS before you close this ticket

If removing Web Site Hosting:

☐ Create a billable ticket to remove Web Site Hosting

☐ Determine where web site will be hosted and who is responsible

- ☐ Work with that person/company to move all html files, database, etc.
- ☐ Test that web site is up and working at new location before you close this ticket

If removing Hosted Email:

- ☐ Create a billable ticket to remove from our Hosted Email service
- ☐ Determine where email should be pointed
- ☐ Work with that person/company to move service
- ☐ Update MX records and other DNS as needed
- ☐ Test that email is flowing before you close this ticket

If removing Email (Spam) Filtering:

- ☐ Create a billable ticket to remove from Spam Filter service
- ☐ Determine where email should be pointed
- ☐ Work with that person/company to move service
- ☐ Update MX records and other DNS as needed
- ☐ Test that email is flowing before you close this ticket

If removing Antivirus:

- ☐ Create a billable ticket to remove from our Antivirus Service
- ☐ NOTE: Be absolutely sure the client understands that we are removing virus protection from their systems!
- ☐ Determine who will be responsible for installing new A-V software
- ☐ Keep that person/company informed as we proceed
- ☐ Notify client and service manager when A-V has been removed

If removing Hosted Storage:

- ☐ Create a billable ticket to remove from our Hosted Storage service
- ☐ Verify that we have a good backup of this data
- ☐ Determine where files need to be copied or moved
- ☐ Determine if an alternative service is to be used. Coordinate with the contact there.
- ☐ Verify that new hosted storage service (or local storage service) is working and that all files are complete before you turn off this service!
- ☐ Backup (or verify that someone else has backed up) all files from the new service before you turn off this service!
- ☐ Notify client and service manager when all files have been moved
- ☐ NOTE: If we can, keep the old service alive for 30 days in case something isn't found.

If removing BDR:

- ☐ Create a billable ticket to remove from BDR service
- ☐ Determine who will be managing BDR going forward
- ☐ Coordinate with them to transfer responsibility for testing service
- ☐ Notify client and service manager when BDR management has been successfully transferred

If removing Microsoft Office (365):

- ☐ Create a billable ticket to remove from Intermedia account
- ☐ Determine how client will access Office going forward
- ☐ If Office is to be installed locally, determine whether this is by us or someone else. If us, include labor on this ticket.
- ☐ If Office is to be delivered via hosted service, work with new provider to transfer users/licenses

If removing Other Services _____ :

- ☐ Create a billable ticket to remove service
- ☐ _____
- ☐ _____
- ☐ _____
- ☐ _____
- ☐ _____

Create a client summary report of all existing issues and tickets. The Service manager will email this to client.

Verify that all documentation is up to date.

Deliver a copy of client documentation to client in paper or electronic format.

Be sure that client has a narrative description of their backup system.

Determine whether any open tickets need to be worked before service is discontinued. Service manager will determine whether each of these is covered by the contract that is ending or is billable.

Close all open tickets for this client that will not be worked. Add a note to each that the ticket was closed without completing service due to end of contract.

When all tickets are closed . . .

- ☐ Remove RMM agents.
- ☐ Log this time in the primary "Exit" ticket
- ☐ Note: unless there is a ticket to set up automatic updates or another service, we are ONLY removing our agents.

☐ Update the daily monitoring documentation so we don't report all those machines as missing.
☐ Update Managed Services Grid

Step Four – Route to Admin Dept.

If the client will be 100% gone, set the expiration date for the Time and Materials contract in the PSA

When all invoices are paid and everything is settled . . .

☐ File all paperwork related to this client.
☐ Remove paper contract(s) for this client from the "current contracts" folder and place in client folder.
☐ Add this completed checklist to client folder

end of checklist

If Needed: Update this checklist!

Last Action:

When all complete, put this form in to filing in-box

Appendix A: Alphabet Soup Cheat Sheet

AC – Alternating Current

AMC – Add, Move, Change. See also MAC.

ASCII – The ASCII Group – ascii.com

AWS – Amazon Web Services

AYCE – All You Can Eat

BAA – Business Associates Agreement (for HIPAA)

BDR – Backup and Disaster Recovery – a device that provides these services

BPOS – Microsoft Business Productivity Online Suite

CALs – Client Access Licenses

CAT-5 (and CAT-6) – Network cabling standards. Category 5 cabling supports up to 1000Base-T or Gigabit Ethernet. Category 6 cabling supports up to 10GBase-T or 10-Gigabit Ethernet.

COGS – Cost of Goods Sold

Colo – Colocation facility or data center

CompTIA – Computing Technology Industry Association – comptia.org

CSP – Cloud Service Provider

GDPR – General Data Protection Regulation (European Union)

GLB – Great Little Book Publishing Co., Inc. I just threw that in to see if anyone reads this stuff.

HaaS – Hardware as a Service

HIPAA – Health Insurance Portability and Accountability Act

IoT – Internet of Things

LOB – Line of Business application

MAC – Move, Add, Change. See also A-M-C.

MDF – Marketing Development Funds

MSA – Managed Service Agreement

MSIAM – *Managed Services in a Month* (book)

MSP – Managed Service Provider

OEM – Original Equipment Manufacturer

PSA – Professional Services Automation

PST - Personal Storage file (used to import/export Outlook data)

QOS – Quality of Service

RMM – Remote Monitoring and Management

RWA – Remote Web Access

SBS – Small Business Server

SKU – Stock Keeping Unit

SMB – Small and Medium Business

SOX – Sarbanes-Oxley Act to protect shareholders

SQL – Structured Query Language

SQL Server – A database standard and the name of a Microsoft server product

TCP/IP – Transmission Control Protocol / Internet Protocol

UNC – Universal Naming Convention

UPS – Uninterruptible Power Supply

VDI – Virtual Desktop Infrastructure

VM – Virtual Machine

VoIP – Voice Over IP

ZDTM – Zero Downtime Migration

Appendix B: Products and Resources Mentioned

Several products are mentioned in this book. A mention is not an endorsement. I'm just presenting the world as I see it. I expect you to take this information, mix in your own experience, see how it fits with your business model, and make your own decisions.

Having said that, it seems silly to mention products and people, but not give the contact information. So here they are in alphabetical order.

I fully acknowledge that links change. So do a little searching if something here no longer works.

ABC Solutions – www.abcsolutionsfl.com

Acronis – www.Acronis.com

Aid4Mail – aid4mail.com/large-scale-email-migration

Alibaba – www.alibabacloud.com/product/oss

Atera – atera.com

Amazon Route 53 - aws.amazon.com/route53

Amazon Web Services – aws.amazon.com

Amazon Web Services Reseller – aws.amazon.com/partners/channel-reseller

AppRiver – appriver.com

ASCII Group – www.ASCII.com

Autotask – www.Autotask.com

Autotask AEM (Datto RMM) – datto.com/business-management/datto-rmm

Auvik – www.auvik.com

Avast – avast.com

AVG antivirus - avg.com

AVG RMM – avg.com/ww-en/managed-workplace

Axcient – www.axcient.com

Azure (Microsoft) – www.WindowsAzure.com

Azure Storage – azure.microsoft.com/en-us/services/storage

Backup Assist - www.backupassist.com

Backup Assist email recovery – backupassist.com/news/exchange-individual-mailbox-backup-and-restore.html

Backupify – from Datto – backupify.com

Barracuda - www.barracuda.com

Barracuda MSP –barracudamsp.com

Bitdefender - bitdefender.com

Brunson, Russell – Author. Books: *Dotcom Secrets* and *Expert Secrets*

Carbonite –carbonite.com

Carr, Nicholas – Author – *The Big Switch*

Cisco Umbrella - umbrella.cisco.com

Click Funnels – www.clickfunnels.com. See also Russell Brunson.

Cloudberry – cloudberrylab.com

Collins, Jim – Author – *Good to Great* and *Great by Choice*

Comodo – comodo.com

CompTIA – Computing Technology Industry Association – www.comptia.org

ConnectWise – www.connectwise.com

Continuum (formerly Zenith Infotech) – www.continuum.net

Datto – datto.com

Direct NIC - DirectNIC.com

DNS Filter - DNSfilter.com

DNS Made Easy - DNSMadeEasy.com

DreamHost - dreamhost.com

Dropbox - dropbox.com

eFolder Anchor –axcient.com/products/anchor

Fat Cow - fatcow.com

GoDaddy - godaddy.com

Google Storage – www.google.com/drive

Great Little Book – www.GreatLittleBook.com

Hostway - hostway.com

Host Gator - hostgator.com

IBM Storage – www.ibm.com/cloud/storage

iDrive –idrive.com/office-365-mailbox-backup

IMAP Move –edoceo.com/creo/imap-move

IMAPsync –imapsync.lamiral.info

Intermedia – www.intermedia.net

Jungle Disk – www.jungledisk.com

Kabuto – repairtechsolutions.com/kabuto/

Kaseya – www.kaseya.com

LabTech (ConnectWise Automate) – labtechsoftware.com

LogicNow – See SolarWinds MSP

Mailprotector – mailprotector.com

Managed Services in a Month – www.ManagedServicesInaMonth.com

Network Solutions - networksolutions.com

Microsoft Azure - www.azure.com

Microsoft OneDrive – onedrive.live.com

Microsoft Office (direct) – office.com

Microsoft Office 365 limits, see: https://docs.microsoft.com/en-us/office365/servicedescriptions/exchange-online-service-description/exchange-online-limits

Ninja RMM – ninjarmm.com

Office365 – products.office.com

OneDrive – onedrive.live.com

Open DNS - opendns.com

Palachuk, Karl – Author

- Books *The Managed Services Operations Manuel* – 4 vol set by Karl W. Palachuk

- Book *The Network Documentation Workbook.*

- Book *The Network Migration Workbook* by Karl W. Palachuk and Manuel Palachuk

- Book *Project Planning in Small Business* by Dana Goulston and Karl W. Palachuk

- Book *Relax Focus Succeed*

- Book *Service Agreements for SMB Consultants: A Quick-Start Guide to Managed Services*

- Book *The Super-Good Project Planner for Technical Consultants*

- Example client training on security – https://www.youtube.com/watch?v=LSRkV4XylRg

- Book *Managed Services in a Month*

QuickBooks (Intuit) – http://quickbooks.intuit.com – QuickBooksOnline.com

Rackspace – www.rackspace.com

Reflexion / Sophos - reflexion.net

Register.com -register.com

Salesforce.com – www. Salesforce.com

Security Training Example: Yutube.com/watch?v=LSRkV4XylRg

Sherweb – www.sherweb.com

Sherweb email restore – https://support.sherweb.com/Faqs/Show/how-to-restore-an-office-365-mailbox-using-online-backup-new

Simpson, Erick – Author

- Book *The Guide to a Successful Managed Services Practice*

- Book *The Best I.T. Sales & Marketing Book Ever!*

- Book *The Best I.T. Service Delivery Book Ever!*

- Book *The Best NOC and Service Desk Operations Book Ever!*

Skykick – skykick.com

Small Biz Thoughts – www.SmallBizThoughts.com – blog. SmallBizThoughts.com – www.smallbizthoughts.org

SMB Books – www.SMBBooks.com

SMB Nation – www.SMBNation.com – Web site, newsletter, and events

SolarWinds Backup – www.solarwindsmsp.com

SolarWinds Mail Assure –solarwindsmsp.com/products/mail

SolarWinds MSP – www.SolarWindsMSP.com

SOP Friday blog posts – www.SOPFriday.com

Sophos - sophos.com

Speedtest.net – Speedtest.net

SRS Plus - srsplus.com

Stable Host - stablehost.com

Storagecraft – storagecraft.com

SyncroMSP – syncromsp.com

Tracy, Brian – Author – *Focal Point.* Book *The 100 Absolutely Unbreakable Laws of Business Success*

Trend Micro - trendmicro.com

Veeam –veeam.com/backup-microsoft-office-365.html

Vipre - vipreantivirus.com

Webroot - webroot.com

Zenith Infotech – See Continuum

Zynstra – www.zynstra.com/proliant-easy-connect/

Classic AD Note: Microsoft is deploying a new kind of AD, based on Azure and intimately tied to their distributed security initiative. They call it Active Directory Domain Services. See https://docs.microsoft.com/en-us/windows-server/identity/ whats-new-active-directory-domain-services. I use the term classic to differentiate the AD model we used from 2000-2018.

Keeping Up With Karl

Karl W. Palachuk is the author of many books, including *The Network Documentation Workbook, Service Agreements for SMB Consultants,* and *The Managed Services Operations Manual.* His first and favorite non-technical book is *Relax Focus Succeed: A Guide to Balancing Your Personal and Professional Lives and Being More Successful with Both.*

Technical Consultant

As Senior Systems Engineer at Small Biz Thoughts, Karl provides technical support to small and medium size businesses in North America. In that role, Karl provides business consulting services and CEO-level training on technical topics. He manages projects and enjoys working with cool technology.

Professional Trainer

As an author, trainer, coach, and blogger, Karl has traveled across the world training technical consultants. His topics have ranged from network documentation to managed services, best practices, and even hiring processes. Karl has been a Microsoft Hands-on-Lab instructor for the Small Business Specialist program.

To view information related to Great Little Book web sites, blog, newsletters, and other information, start at

www.SmallBizThoughts.com

Other Stuff

Sign Up for Karl's Email List!

www.SMBBooks.com

This list covers upcoming events, seminars, news, and "what's happening" in the SMB Consulting space. Very low volume. One email a week and fewer than ten other emails throughout the year.

Motivational Trainer – Relax Focus Succeed

Meanwhile, over in the world of *Relax Focus Succeed*, Karl is also an author, newsletter writer, and trainer. The goal of RFS is to learn how to balance your personal and professional lives and become more successful in both.

To view information related to Relax Focus Succeed web sites, blog, newsletters, and other information, start at

www.relaxfocussucceed.com

Speaker

If you are interested in having Karl present to your group, or do a training at your office, please contact him:

Karl W. Palachuk

www.KarlPalachuk.com

Email: karlp@smallbizthoughts.com

More Great Books on Managed Services.

For more information, visit **www.smbbooks.com**.

Service Agreements for SMB Consultants

A Quick-Start Guide to Managed Services

by Karl W. Palachuk

This award-winning best seller does a lot more than give you sample agreements.

Karl starts out with a discussion of how you run your business and the kinds of clients you want to have. The combination of these – defining yourself and defining your clients – is the basis for your service agreements.

Service agreements are not about service – they're about relationships.

The Managed Services Operations Manual – 4 vol. set

by Karl W. Palachuk

Standard Operating Procedures for Computer Consultants and Managed Service Providers

Every computer consultant, every managed service provider, every technical consulting company - every successful business - needs SOPs!

When you document your processes and procedures, you design a way for your company to have repeatable success. And as you fine-tune those processes and procedures, you become more successful, more efficient, and more profitable.

Relax Focus Succeed®

Balance Your Personal and Professional Lives and Become More Successful in Both

by Karl W. Palachuk

The premise of this book is simple but powerful: The fundamental keys to success are focus, hard work, and balance. Too often, the advice we receive gives plenty of attention to focus and hard work, but very little to balance.

Managed Services in a Month – 3rd edition

by Karl W. Palachuk

The Complete Guide to Successful IT Consulting

The best-selling book ever on the topic of Managed Services – from one of the pioneers of the managed services business model.

It's not too late to get into managed services. In fact, Karl argues, it's the business model of the future. No matter what else you do, you need to learn how to be extremely successful with a maintenance-based recurring revenue model.

Index

B

C

N

O

P

T

U

V

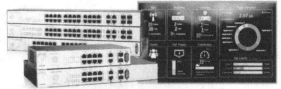

datto

Powering Smarter Managed Services

Revenue Generating Services

- Unified Continuity
- Networking
- SaaS Protection
- File Backup & Sync

Business Management Tools

- Professional Services Automation (PSA)
- Remote Monitoring & Management (RMM)

datto.com

The IT Community

5 REASONS
TO JOIN ASCII TODAY

The premier community of North American MSPs, VARs & solution providers

PROGRAMS

Gain access to our 70+ programs and services as well as a dedicated membership representative. Pick and choose the programs that work for your company.

ADVOCACY

We are your advocate in the industry. If there is an issue with a partner, contact us. ASCII will reach out on your behalf and often get the issue resolved in one email.

COMMUNITY

The ASCII Group is a community...we are vendor agnostic and do not require the use of any particular vendor or service.

SAVINGS

Our business programs provide an excellent ROI – more than offsetting your cost of membership. We offer distributor, manufacturer and business service discounts.

OPPORTUNITY

Our group has over $9.6 Billion in system wide sales that we leverage for your benefit. We also have private group buys and offer competitive business insurance programs.

Use promo code KARL when joining to receive **2 free months** on top of your first year of membership

Phone: 800-394-2724 | E-mail: trevor@ascii.com | URL: www.ascii.com

CPSIA information can be obtained
at www.ICGtesting.com
Printed in the USA
BVHW080855040619
550105BV00014B/716/P

9 781942 115540